Anne Sparrowhawk

Social Networking for Seniors

in easy steps

For the Over 50s

In easy steps is an imprint of In Easy Steps Limited
Southfield Road · Southam
Warwickshire CV47 0FB · United Kingdom
www.ineasysteps.com

Notice of Liability
Every effort has been made to ensure that this book contains accurate
and current information. However, In Easy Steps Limited and the
author shall not be liable for any loss or damage suffered by readers
as a result of any information contained herein.

Trademarks
All trademarks are acknowledged as belonging to their respective
companies.

In Easy Steps Limited supports The Forest Stewardship Council (FSC),
the leading international forest certification organisation. All our titles
that are printed on Greenpeace approved FSC certified paper carry the
FSC logo.

MIX
Paper from
responsible sources
FSC www.fsc.org   FSC® C020837

Printed and bound in the United Kingdom

ISBN 978-1-84078-410-7

Contents

1 What is Social Networking?

This chapter outlines what social networking is all about, introduces the main concepts, and explodes some of the popular myths.

Why this book?

Social networking has become a phrase widely used in the media and, at one time, it used to refer to social gatherings where you might meet like-minded people. You had to be in the same place at the same time in order to take part.

In recent years, the development of services on the Internet has meant that the term 'social networking' now has a completely new connotation. It's all about connecting with people via the computer and the Internet, wherever those people may be, to share a common interest or purpose.

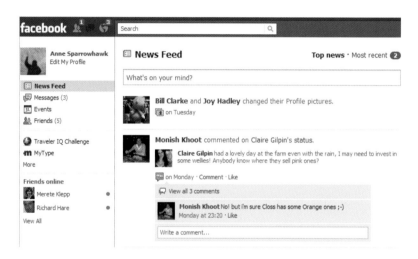

Social networking has certainly had a major impact on the younger generation. The growth of sites like MySpace and Facebook has been extremely rapid, and the vast majority of students under the age of 25 are likely to be active users.

This book is designed to help those of us who are past the first flush of youth to understand what the hype is all about.

In particular, this book will help you to:

- choose the social network or networks that you can engage with

- understand the processes you will need to follow

- walk through the joining and publishing processes

- understand the terminology

- dispel some of the myths about social networking

- understand the implications of some of the steps you are invited to take

- manage your accounts so that you can control your own data

- use social networking sites to enhance your life, not have them control you!

Hot tip

If you have friends or relatives on a site, asking them what they use it for might give you a helpful starting point.

Beware

Start slowly – don't expect to be running groups using a site too quickly!

What is social networking for?

The main purpose of social networking sites is to give you tools that make it possible for you to communicate effectively with different groups of people in your social circle. You can choose what types of communication you want to make, and with whom.

Who do you want to communicate with?

- You can keep in contact with family members on a gap year, or away at university

- You could use a network to run a sports team, a book group or an association, so all the members can find out what is planned

- You can find new people to communicate with about an interest you share

- You can find people you have lost touch with

- You can set up your own community and run projects, or activities, using it

- You can use the network to find out what's going on - this might be on your favorite celebrities' website, or in the area of a particular hobby or industry

What form will the communication take?

How you interact with other people varies from site to site. In many cases, the communications made are very quick and easy to carry out.

- They might be comments about how you are feeling, what you are doing, or where you are

- They might be longer pieces of writing, thoughts, or ideas

- Some sites offer very specific formats for the information they are looking for, and support you in writing a book or film review, or comments on restaurants or hotels visited

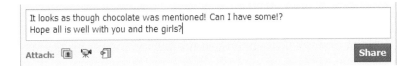

It looks as though chocolate was mentioned! Can I have some!?
Hope all is well with you and the girls?

Attach: **Share**

- Give information about the work you do and have done in the past

- Some sites specifically support pictures or video, allowing you to load them into a site and let other people view and comment on them

11

flickr from YAHOO!

Home   You ▾   Organize & Create ▾   Contacts ▾   Groups ▾   Explore ▾

Your photostream   44 items / 27 views

Sets   Galleries   Tags   People   Archives   Favorites   Popular   Profile

NanaGodfredArhin

click here to add a description

©   ☐   Only friends can see this photo (**edit**)

RockyAcquah

click here to add a description

©   ☐   Only friends can see this photo (**edit**)

Social networking myths

Beware

Try not to listen to those people who want to put you off because they don't use social networking sites themselves.

"Once you're on a social networking site, you'll spend all your time doing it."

Well, this is up to you! Some people have said the same about email, and perhaps you now know that's not true. Of course, there's not much point in going to all the trouble of setting up an account if you are only going to use it very occasionally. It will require some of your time, but how much definitely depends on yourself.

"I won't understand what's going on."

That's why you're reading this book! If you can access the Internet and find websites you want to visit, you can certainly use a social networking site. There are different cultures associated with different sites, but, once you become familiar with them, you will not find it difficult.

"I'll lose my privacy."

Every social networking site has ways of making sure you share personal data, like your email address, age, telephone number and so on, ONLY with the people you choose to share it with. Taking time to understand how the profile system works will make sure that this is the case.

"When I've got a social network profile everyone will contact me."

It all depends how you use the site, and how your friends use it too. You can decide who you link to, and who you allow to link to you, so how big your network of friends becomes is entirely up to you.

"I don't have the computer skills to use social networking sites."

As long as you can access the Internet and use email you will be technically able to use a social networking site. It really is not difficult.

Who is really there?

As you will see as you work through this book, I have created a number of different alter egos as accounts, to use as illustrations. Other people can do that too - so it is appropriate to be aware that people may not always be who they say they are!

Usually, when you set up your site, you will be asked to give an email address that the site 'belongs' to. This provides some security, as there is a notifiable person behind the content, though, of course, this is not a great level of accountability.

Beware

It is true that not everyone will be who they say they are. Read contributions with a sensible amount of skepticism – and don't take everything too seriously.

Personalize Skype

Show off your WeeMee to the world.
Build your free Weemee.

Identity is central to some sites – Friends Reunited, where you are trying to contact people from your past, or Skype, where you want to talk to particular people. It would be pointless to represent yourself as someone different on those sites. However, it is sometimes sensible to use two different identities to distinguish between yourself at work and at leisure – you might not want work colleagues to share your list of friends or your personal interests, so creating two different profiles within one network might be a way around that.

You would not give your phone number to any casual acquaintance you meet in the street or the mall. You should be no more or less cautious with interactions on social network sites.

Sharing information

There's a range of different information that you can share when you join a social networking site.

Factual information about you

- This is the personal information about yourself - your profile or homepage. It often includes your birthday

- A photograph of yourself - some sites encourage users to use a cartoon or animated character to represent themselves. This is particularly the case if the site supports children

- Most sites have a format that includes your personal profile, sometimes called your Account, Home, Profile. The personal information you put here will be shared widely with people accessing the site.

Information that is the focus of the site

- This might be where you are, what you are doing, what you think, how you feel, where you are going next. It might be a range of photographs, or something specific about an event or activity

- The site will offer you a text space to write in, or might offer a range of choices for you to select one or more. The site handles all the formatting, so the information is well-presented when it appears on-screen

Readers of the site can comment or give feedback about the information you have supplied. If it concerns them - for example, if it identifies them as a family member - they will be asked to confirm the relationship, sometimes before it appears on the site.

 Jonathan Moller accepted your family request.
on Tuesday

Don't forget

Write down your user name and password somewhere and keep it safe. You will want to check it at some time in the future.

14

Keeping safe

Some media sources make a lot about the dangers of social networking sites, but, provided you are sensible, it is most unlikely that your information will be compromised. There are a few simple rules to follow - and to make sure the young people you know also follow.

Beware

Photos that show people in compromising situations might be used against them, and you too.

- Be very cautious about giving your phone number and address to anyone, especially by publishing it to your profile

- Don't ever give away your logon details and password - even to a friendly colleague

- Consider carefully the pictures you use for your profile and in other contexts on the site. Could they be misused?

	Everyone	Friends of friends	Friends only
My status, photos, and posts			•
Bio and favorite quotations	•		
Family and relationships			•
Photos and videos I'm tagged in			•
Religious and political views			•
Birthday			•

- Make sure you set the security options on the site, and start them at the most secure settings. It's easier to take some filters off than to put them back on

- If you access your site at a computer used by others, make sure you log out of any social networking site you have been using properly (and email sites too)

- Once something has been published on one of these sites, it's difficult to remove it. Make sure you have followed the advice in this book, and have also used your common sense before publishing sensitive pictures and information online.

Beware

If other people have copied material that you regret placing on the site, those copies will still exist even if you remove your original.

15

'Lurking' and taking part

There's a vast amount of material to read and explore on networking sites. A good way to find out what it's all about, and to work out how you want to use the site, is to spend a bit of time having a look around. You might want to read what people are saying, look at some pages, find people you know, identify some games or activities that you want to join. When you do all of these things without writing anything, it's called 'lurking'. It's completely fine to do that, and, in fact, it's the best way of getting to understand how a range of other people use the site.

Some sites offer a number of approaches for exploring. For example, this is a starting page from Flickr.

Explore interesting photos on Flickr by choosing a point in time...

Select a month

Choose ▼

More places to explore:

- Interesting photos from the last 7 days
- Calendar view of this month
- A map of the world
- Camera Finder
- Most recent uploads
- Video on Flickr
- Galleries
- The App Garden
- The Flickr Blog

When you do start taking part, you will find that you start to get messages back from people you have interacted with. They may be agreeing to link to you, or telling you that they have left you a message. You will often get an email to tell you that a message has been received. This will be found in the email box you had used as a reference when you signed up for the site.

Once you have joined up and started to take part, the contributions you make will start to build up somewhere.

 Anne Sparrowhawk Photographs from a fantastic weeke on the Shetland Islands and especially Unst with Jonathan 17th and 20th August 2007.
 Tagged: Jonathan Moller

Anne Sparrowhawk
44 new photos

 21 August 2007 at 19:01 · Comment · Like · Share

> **Ebenezer Amoh** there is very nice place
> 11 March at 17:13 · Like · Delete

Write a comment...

This is an example of an entry into my Facebook page dating back several years, and you can see how comments from a reader have also been saved.

Don't forget

You can usually remove materials you have put up on the site.

17

Copyright issues

Once your writing, pictures, photographs and so on are posted onto a website, they are very easy to copy. But just because something is copiable, it does not mean that it is copyright free. This is a complex legal area. Make sure you are legal by posting pictures on sites that are your own. Sites often have comments in the 'fine print', such as:

"you grant us a non-exclusive, transferable, sub-licensable, royalty-free, worldwide license to use any IP content that you post on or in connection with" Facebook.

That specifically means that Facebook can hold the image referred to, and other people that you have allowed to go to your Facebook page can see it. They can also copy it if they choose to and use it on their page. This is the area in which control can potentially slip away if you do not have your privacy settings tight enough.

Once images have appeared on the Internet it can be difficult to control them, so it's important to consider whether you want your pictures to be shared with such a wide audience. Each site has its own rules, and these are discussed in the chapters that follow.

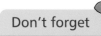

Don't forget

You will not have a record of who has seen your page and copied your images.

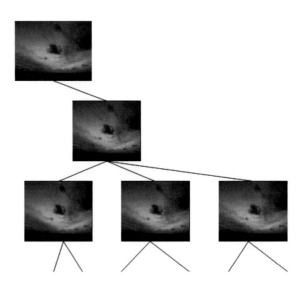

What you need to start

The basic tools for social networking are:

- A computer or a Smartphone

- An Internet connection

- An email address

The computer

Social networking sites are all online, so they are available to you from whichever computer you happen to be using. All the information you enter when you set up your account for a site is kept in some computer somewhere, but you do not have to know exactly where. When you log in to the site, it will know about you, and allow you to access your materials from wherever you happn to be. If you are at home, at work, in the library, visiting another country, your social network can be accessed by you from any computer linked to the Internet.

When you connect to the Internet, you view sites through a browser - a piece of software that sits on your computer and interprets websites so that you can see them. There are a number of different browsers; Internet Explorer, Mozilla Firefox, and Google Chrome are the most common ones on the PC platform, with Apple's Safari being most widespread on the Apple. The browsers are updated from time to time, and, if your computer is using an old browser, you might consider downloading a more recent version to get a better experience of social networking.

Smartphones can also access social networking sites, and this will be discussed in some of the following chapters.

The Internet connection

The Internet connection might be a dial-up or on broadband. You cannot tell the difference by looking at the computer or the telephone socket, but the speed of response will make that very clear! If it takes a very long time for pages to load from the Internet, then the chances are you are using a dial-up connection rather than broadband. This will also be very tedious when you are uploading pictures.

Beware

A dial up connection ties up the phone line as long as you are online. Charges may increase after you have been online for 60 minutes, too.

Don't forget

You will need to know your user name and password when you access a site from a computer you have not logged on from before.

...cont'd

An email account

You've probably got an email address already. Social networking sites usually require you to have one, so that they can authorise your account. They often send information about updates to their software, or send you messages to let you know that someone has contacted you. If you don't have an email address, then some sites won't let you join at all.

You can create a new email address and link all your new social networks to it. This can be useful, especially if you want to keep work and social life separate. You can register to have an email with many different organizations. Here's a few of the most common ones.

www.googlemail.com

www.yahoo.com

www.msn.com

www.hotmail.com

All of these offer free email accounts, and a certain amount of webspace too. They all rely on a browser as the way to access the account, but will generally operate on a wide range of browsers, even quite old ones.

So now you are ready!

So, with a computer, Internet connection and email account prepared, you are ready to join a network. The next section discusses some of the ways you can choose which one to join.

2 Purposes of Social Networking

This chapter gives an overview of the sites, so you can choose which to join.

Types of social network

There are significant overlaps between most of the different social networks, with many common features they share. Having said this, it is also true that each site has a particular focus and purpose it serves, and being clear what you want to do will help you choose the right network to suit your needs.

Social networking sites could be sorted into four different groups for different purposes.

Hot tip

Don't join lots of different networks at once. Choose one to explore more fully, to start with.

- To help you connect with friends you already know, and make new ones too.

  Facebook, MySpace, BeBo, Friends Reunited and Hi5 are the main sites that fall into this group

- To help you connect with specialist communities that share a particular interest

  Saga Zone, LinkedIn, Plaxo and Ning are the most well known sites that fulfil this need

- To help you present your ideas or resources in a form that can be shared on the Internet

  Flickr for photographs, YouTube for videos, and Blogger or WordPress for writing blogs

- To help you find out what is going on in whatever sphere of activity that interests you

  Twitter is the best known information sharing site, but there are a number of others, such as Delicious and Digg.com, who all keep their users up-to-date. Meetup and TripIt support people who want to physically meet other people that share an interest, or traveling to the same area.

The rest of this chapter describes these networks in some detail, which should allow you to make some choices about which network or networks you want to start exploring.

Connecting with friends

This is the simplest sort of social network to understand and, in many ways to join too. The site you join will mostly depend on who you want to talk to. If all of your contacts use Facebook, then this is the obvious choice. If instead they are using MySpace, Bebo or Hi5, then that will be the site you need to join.

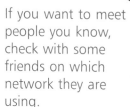

Hot tip

If you want to meet people you know, check with some friends on which network they are using.

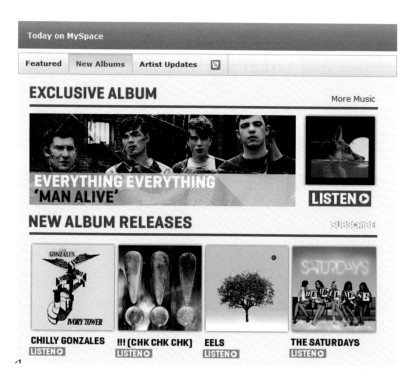

MySpace

This is the screen you can visit on MySpace.com without logging on. As you can see, a considerable focus for this site is the music and entertainment industry. When you link to individual pages, you will find that users have created their own designs for their pages. They can look very different, allowing an individuality that other sites do not support.

The screenshots that follow reflect some of the different types of design style users have applied to their pages.

...cont'd

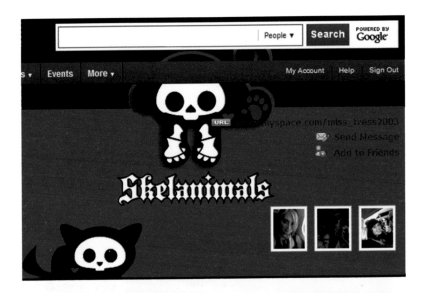

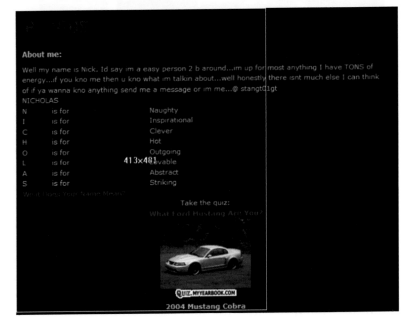

As you can see, both of these users have chosen very different page styles to reflect themselves and their interests. The site is particularly good for users who want to upload their music and sound files, and for finding out about new releases or festival playlists.

...cont'd

Facebook

This is a typical Facebook.com page, with content specific to that person (in this case, a group) together with information on their 'wall'. The idea of the wall is that it's a place people write on – the person themselves as well as others. The most recent things to have been written, called 'posts' are at the top of the screen and older information can be read as you scroll down the page. The following is a list of some of the activities you can carry out on Facebook:

- Create a profile for yourself
- Post photographs and tag them with the names of people in the shots
- Comment about events
- Play games and invite others to compete with you
- Set up surveys
- List your favorite films, books or music
- Set up group sites to support your club or organization

When you log into the site, a page of 'News' will be presented to you, giving you information about the things your contacts have been doing, for you to comment on.

Beware

Never put your telephone number or full address on the information about you – it is open for everyone to read if you post it there.

25

...cont'd

FriendsReunited.com or classmates.com

If you are trying to find some friends and contacts from the past, then you might be better off joining Friends Reunited or classmates.com, which are set up with the specific purpose of helping you find friends from school, college or previous workplaces. These sites offer links to schools, colleges, universities and, increasingly, work places.

Don't forget

It is important to enter the year you were at the school. Some of the schools have thousands of pupil records.

These networks are very specific in their purpose and, therefore, make it easy to find schools and so on by having comprehensive lists to choose from.

If you are becoming interested in finding out about your family tree and ancestors, similar sorts of sites are available to make that process easier. Genesreunited.co.uk is a site related to Friends Reunited; there are others, such as Geni. com, ancestry.com or ancestry.co.uk, and genealogy.com.

Specialist communities

Specialist communities generally have a defined purpose. LinkedIn and Plaxo are specifically designed to support the business community, whilst SagaZone is directed at the over 50s. There are sites for book enthusiasts, artists, music buffs, and so on. If those specialisms interest you, try:

www.goodreads.com

www.artition.com

www.last.fm

Don't forget

There are lots of different sites for subject interests, and a google search will be a good place to start.

LinkedIn

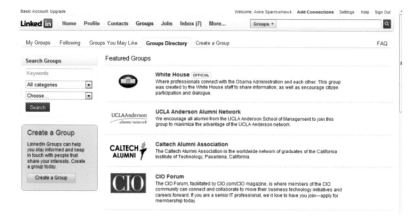

This is an example of a page from LinkedIn.com that illustrates the look and feel of the site. Its focus is on providing a site you can use to describe your work, career, skills, and ambitions. It uses its engine to then present you with people you might know or want to link with. It offers opportunities to form groups of like-minded people or people with a particular focus and interest. It also offers a jobs page. The site, in its basic form, is free, but you can also upgrade to a variety of services, to gain introductions to people within particular companies that you might be interested in for example.

This is a community that particularly supports people involved in business and consultancy work, and is developing additional services all the time.

...cont'd

Plaxo

Plaxo.com is a service designed to manage contact details and addresses for business needs and also for family life. It is set up with data fields, supporting the user in saving both work data and family data as separate sets of information. It allows you to link to mail lists that you have in your email address book, so you can keep one set of contacts and know that it will always be current.

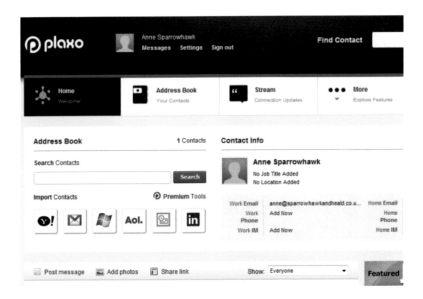

This site also offers you the opportunity to upgrade to a monthly professional subscription. If you choose to do that, then the site offers opportunities to synchronise your data across different services as well as with your phone. It also offers an internal message service called ProMail, which allows you to communicate directly with other Plaxo users.

Both Plaxo and LinkedIn are really focused at the professional user, with some additional features that make the service more personal - book recommendations within LinkedIn for example; adding photos into a gallery on Plaxo. The sense of community created on both of these sites comes about through grouping of people and with tools to facilitate discussion. The sites serve their business or data management purpose rather than offering a community site as a resource you might want to dip into for interest or entertainment.

Saga Zone

SagaZone.co.uk is a site that has been developed by an organization that specifically supports the over 50s. There are no serious checks to make sure younger people do not join. This is the community part of a magazine site that has a wide range of published information, planned to be of particular interest to this age group. There's information on travel, finance, health and lifestyle, as well as a link to the community site.

Hot tip

The magazine part of this site has lots of interesting articles that you might want to discuss on Saga Zone. www.sagazone.co.uk

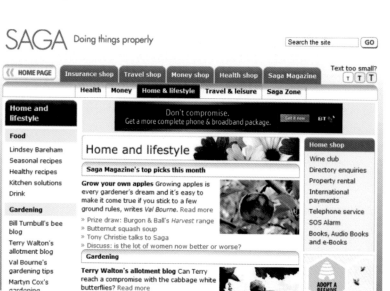

Beware

Younger friends are unlikely to find their way to your really interesting blog here!

Saga Zone offers profiling, forums, clubs that you can set up, areas where you can write a blog or create a library of your pictures. Central to the benefits of this site is the fact that the audience is narrower than on other social networking sites, so it can be easier to find like minds to communicate with.

Sharing your ideas

You can, of course, share your ideas on many sites, and, as we've already seen, this can range from quite short messages and comments to longer blogs. A number of sites also allow you to share and structure your photographs.

If you want to write signficantly more, or manage a large collection of images or videos, then there are a number of specialist sites you should consider using.

Flickr

Flickr.com is probably the best known site for managing images, and also short videos. Videos are a relatively new feature, and there are limits to the size of video that can be uploaded.

As well as being a site where you can store large numbers of photographs, the main features Flickr offers are to do with the process of structuring your photo collection. When you upload photographs, you can tag them in a variety of ways - event, date, people involved, location and so on. You can also make them available for private view, so that only people you choose to view your pictures can see them.

Don't forget

You can upload your digital images to lots of different places, if you want to.

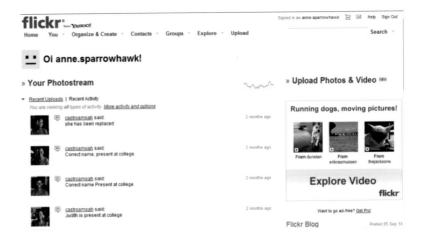

When you have organized your pictures, you can then invite others to view them, and encourage feedback and discussion about the images and the events or activities they show.

...cont'd

YouTube

YouTube.com is the best known site for managing video, and has access to a vast range of other videos; all sorts of music, TV shows, festivals, sporting events, news, educational resources, and science and technology sections.

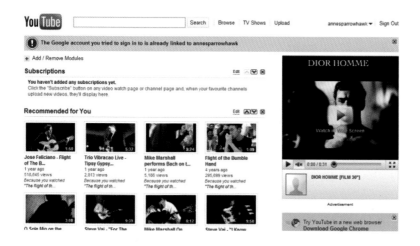

You can view missed episodes of TV shows, or, if you find that there is a video provider that you find particularly interesting, you can subscribe to his account and when you subsequently return to YouTube all of his new videos will be offered to you.

You can very easily upload your own videos to the site - anything up to 15 minutes in length or smaller than 2GB in size. The site also provides a tool for uploading longer videos too. You can also link videos you provide directly to other community sites – Facebook and Twitter, for example.

The site provides a number of tools for managing videos you may find interesting – these include creating playlists of your favorites, and sharing these as channels for others to play and enjoy. This is really helpful as a way of making sure that you can find videos that you really enjoyed again.

Beware

Uploading video can take a long time, even if you have broadband. Upload times are always longer than download!

Beware

YouTube is strict about making sure that you only upload videos that you have the rights to.

Don't forget

You can link videos from YouTube to other community sites.

...cont'd

Tools for blogging

If you want to write signficantly more than the average site allows, then you will need to choose a site that will provide you with a blogging tool. There are a number of these available, some of which give you more or less control over the way in which your blog looks, and where it is stored.

If you want to use a blogging tool that provides you with web space as well as the tool, then any of the following would be a good choice:

- www.wordpress.com

  This site provides fixed templates, and allows you to categorize your site so that others can find it

- www.blogger.com

  Provided by Google, this site allows you to customize your template easily, and lets you categorize your posts

- www.livejournal.com

  This is a more community organized blog site, where, as its name suggests, the focus can be more on a record of how you are and what you are thinking about

- www.wordpress.org

  This differs from its sister site (wordpress.com) in that it allows you to download the blogging software and then install it on your own webspace

Some of the community sites provide you with a blogging tool and web space. Facebook, for example, has a 'Notes' space that can be viewed by your friends.

The audience you find for your blog will, of course, depend on where it is placed. The blog on the next page, for example, comes from Saga Zone and will, therefore, only be read by Saga Zone members.

In this case, the author has disabled the comments feature, but most bloggers welcome feedback from their audience.

Don't forget

You can use lots of sites to blog; some offer you more control of how your blog looks than others.

Hot tip

Think carefully about who you want to read your blog, and how they will find out about it. That will help you decide where it should be on the Internet.

...cont'd

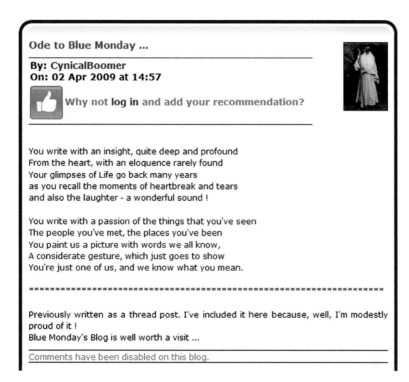

Ode to Blue Monday ...

By: CynicalBoomer
On: 02 Apr 2009 at 14:57

Why not **log in** and add your recommendation?

You write with an insight, quite deep and profound
From the heart, with an eloquence rarely found
Your glimpses of Life go back many years
as you recall the moments of heartbreak and tears
and also the laughter - a wonderful sound !

You write with a passion of the things that you've seen
The people you've met, the places you've been
You paint us a picture with words we all know,
A considerate gesture, which just goes to show
You're just one of us, and we know what you mean.

✖✖✖

Previously written as a thread post. I've included it here because, well, I'm modestly proud of it !
Blue Monday's Blog is well worth a visit ...

Comments have been disabled on this blog.

The following blog was created in Blogger.com and gives a flavor of the design and features that the blog site offers. Comments from readers, links to followers or members, links to other community sites, such as Facebook and Twitter, are all built in once you choose the software.

Beware

A public blog can be read by anyone. Make sure you don't write private information by mistake.

Find out what's going on

The use of social networking sites as a means of finding out what people are doing, where they are, and what they are thinking has become a really popular activity amongst many groups. Some of the sites already discussed have this as part of their purpose. The group of sites described here have sharing current information as their primary purpose.

Sites like Twitter, Delicious, Meetup, Tripit have all contributed to different sorts of shared information. Of them all, Twitter is probably the most commonly mentioned. Famous authors, politicians, comedians and other celebrities all use Twitter as a means of keeping in touch with their fan base, but lots of professionals and individuals use Twitter as a way of sharing what they are doing and learning.

Twitter

Beware

The 140 character limit is real! A post that is any longer than that will just be cut off.

Twitter – www.twitter.com – rose to prominence through its restriction to 140 characters per posting. In the example above, you can see that there are links to websites or further information to explore. These can be very powerful as ways of linking information to a wider audience. People attending conferences, exhibitions or eating at restaurants can share their experiences with others. In Twitter, this is called creating a Tweet. When you have found people who have interesting things to share, you can choose to be a 'follower'. That means that each time you log on to the site, new postings from them will be listed for you. You can ask them questions directly, and also pass their information on to others – Retweeting. There are some people who spend a lot of their time creating Tweets, and others who are Followers. It is a great resource as a site for gauging the reaction to current events, or attitudes to situations. The widespread use of Smartphones has made Twitter a very practical site for communicating when traveling, giving users a feel for what is happening 'right now'.

Delicious

As well as sharing experiences electronically with people, it is often useful to share website resources you found solved a problem or answered a particular question. Delicious.com was set up specifically to provide that service. People from all sorts of walks of life save their weblinks to the website and allow others to share them.

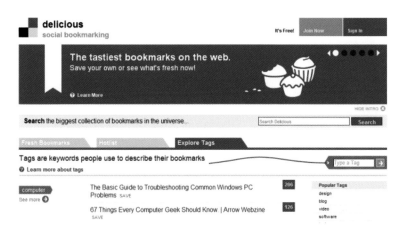

This can be really useful if you start working in a new area, or field of interest. It can be a quick way of finding a set of relevant documents or information. Following particular people can also help to find websites of common interest.

Don't forget

Your interesting site choices might be of value to others, so don't forget to contribute as well as follow.

...cont'd

Reditt.com

This is a site where people can share the information they have found on the Internet. Site members choose the stories that are most interesting to them. As they choose the stories, popular ones rise to the top, and are then shown on the 'Front Page'. The arrows next to the story show how many people have read it.

Digg.com

This is a site that is similar to Reditt, with perhaps more focus on issues of a political nature. Comments can be added to the news link, and, if you share the view of the person commenting, you can show that by adding your positive vote – a Digg.

Meeting people

As well as sharing experiences electronically with people, most of us have a need to actually physically meet with people to be sociable. There is, of course, a lot of media concern about using social networking sites to meet people, but, if you follow some sensible guidelines, this can be a really valuable experience. There are a couple of tools designed specifically to support you physically meeting people rather than just electronically.

TripIt

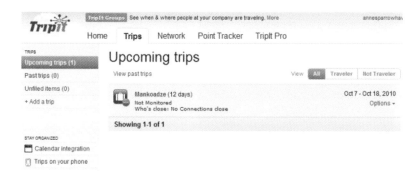

Tripit.com offers a tool that allows you to find out about the travel plans of people you know and contact through email, and where they might be right now. You can arrange groups or just provide information about your own travels. Anyone linked to you through this service will be notified when your travel plans coincide.

This can be a useful way of keeping in touch with people who travel a lot. When you set up your account you can choose the people you inform through TripIt, so that you only inform those people you might really want to meet up with.

Beware

It is easy to select all your email addresses and keep them all informed about your plans – but it's worth checking that you really do want your plumber and stationery supplier to be included!

...cont'd

Meetup

Meetup.com is a site that is designed to help you meet people who share a common interest. It does so by helping users find a Meetup group nearby, or to start a new one. The starting point for the site is your area of interest and your location.

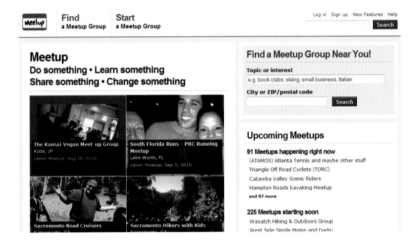

Once you have entered your location you will be able to see the Meetups already arranged in your area. You can then join and choose to attend a meeting, using the site to communicate with the Meet organizer. All the usual web conventions apply – profiles, feedback, discussions, photos and so on.

This chapter has provided a broad overview of the different social networks available, and presented some suggestions as to the purpose and focus of each. In the next chapter we will be exploring some of the basic concepts in a little more detail, so that, if you want to join networks that have not been detailed in this book, you will be prepared for the processes to follow, ensuring that your social networking experience is positive and trouble-free.

3 Basic Concepts and Accounts

Social networks mostly follow similar processes for joining and setting up your account.

Creating an account

To get started, you need to get to the site, by either typing the web address into your browser, or by doing a search for Facebook or YouTube, for example.

The first thing you need to do to be an active member of a social network is to register as a user and create an account. All the sites explored in this book offer a free account service. Some of them encourage you to take a paid subscription and, for that, offer you more services, but, in the first instance, you can explore the site and how it works for free. You can decide whether you want to become a paid up member later.

When you get to the home page for the social networking site you will find an invitation to open an account – it might be Create an Account, Join, Sign Up. It will usually be near the top of the screen. Once you click on that, you will be invited to enter information into a number of forms. Exactly what is required will vary from one service to the next, but most ask for the following.

- An email address: This lets the network communicate with you about your account, and also tells you when people have commented on what you have written. Your account will usually only be valid when the site has sent you an email, and you have responded to it (see next page)

- A password: Ideally a combination of letters, numbers and punctuation works best. There's usually a restriction on needing at least 6 and sometimes 8 characters. A word where you replace the o with 0, a with 4 and e with 3 leads to a strong password – and one you might remember!

- Username: This has to be unique, and some sites will offer you a suggestion of an available name based on what you have typed in

Hot tip

Write your passwords and user names down somewhere only you can find them.

Beware

If you disguise your age by thinking of a false birthday, make sure you write it down somewhere, to remember it. (Also be aware that others may have done the same!)

- Date of birth: This is often used as a check piece of information by the website, if you have lost your account information. Some sites use it publicly, and friends can then be reminded to send you a message on the day. It can also help make sure you are talking to the **right person**

Security checks

Usually most sites want to make sure that you are a human being and not a spammer. To do this, they ask you to read some squiggly writing called a Captcha – you can listen to the letters being spoken to you, if you prefer.

Hot tip

Sometimes the squiggly letters are really hard to read. You can ask for another set. Check whether they are case sensitive or not, too.

Once you have successfully done that, the service will usually give you a message telling you to go to your email account.

Hot tip

Sometimes the link in the email doesn't work. You then need to copy the full address link into your browser.

You need to go to your email account and click on the link in the message. This ensures that you are indeed the owner of the email you used to register the account.

Hi, Anne!

Thanks for joining MySpace!

Confirm your MySpace account

Here's your account info for logging in:

41

Creating your profile

When you become an active user of a social networking site, you will want to find people who have similar interests. Perhaps, to start with, you only want to talk to friends and family that you already know. In that case, your profile is important as a way of making sure that you are talking with the right person. However unusual your name, you are almost certain to find that there is someone else on the network who shares it.

Your age and general location might be provided automatically, but there is a variety of additional information that you can choose to supply.

Where I grew up	Where I live now	Places I've lived
What I do	Current company	Companies I've worked for
Examples: Actor, Engineer, Scientist	Current school	Schools I've attended

Verified domains
You have verified email addresses at the following domains. Check which domains you'd like to appear on your profile. Your email addresses will not be displayed. This will help visitors to your profile know that you are the real you. Learn more

☐ sparrowhawkandheald.co.uk   Verify another email address

A little personality

Short bio B I U ≡ ≣ ∞	Something I can't find using Google
	Examples: paradise, love, Atlantis, Oceanic 815, spam
	My superpower
	Examples: flying, teleportation, time travel, eating chips and salsa
	Interests
	Examples: backpacking, astronomy, travel, photography, cooking

Some of the information will only be available to people you have specifically authorized to read it. Other information will be there for all to read, so do think about that when you are entering text. This is an area teachers might want to be particularly aware of when they write things that students might read.

Social networks make use of the user profile in different ways, as will become clear in the following chapters of this book. If you are exploring a new network, look at other users to see how they have used the profiling, and decide what you think will work best for you.

Your profile image

Nearly every social network gives you the opportunity to use an image of yourself. This is genuinely helpful as a way of making sure that you are talking or communicating with the right person. So it's definitely best if the picture looks like you. However, do not assume that everyone uses their own picture. There are certainly many who do not, some with an intention to deceive.

The picture is usually quite small, and the site will generally reduce the image to be the right size. It is best to start off with a head and shoulders image, though it does not have to be as serious and formal as a passport photo. It's a good idea to have a plain background behind you, and also to stick with it for some time, as changing it frequently might confuse your readers.

You can reduce pictures down to about 350 pixels across, which will suit most sites. This will make the picture quicker to load.

Alternatively, you can use a site like www.weeworld.com to create a passable cartoon version of yourself, like this example here.

Once you have created or found an image that you like, it can be used across a range of different networking sites. There might be a benefit in having a different image for a site you use professionally, as opposed to one for social purposes only, but otherwise consistency has a real benefit.

Hot tip

Choose an image that is recognizable but would not make a good passport photo. Then you can be sure the image will never be used for identity theft.

Don't forget

There is not a limit to the number of different accounts you can have. It is good practice to have one for 'work' related activity and another for social things.

Managing your identity

There are a number of different ways you can ensure that you do not have difficulties with your profile and identity on social networking sites. Sites generally have a menu option somewhere about Privacy. It will give you specific information about how you can make sure that your information is shared with people you want to share it with, and not with others.

	Everyone	Friends of friends	Friends only
My status, photos, and posts			•
Bio and favorite quotations	•		
Family and relationships			•
Photos and videos I'm tagged in			•
Religious and political views			•
Birthday			•
Can comment on posts			•
Places I check in to [?]			•
Contact information			•

This is the privacy setting information from Facebook. It has three different groups of people who can see your information. 'Friends only' is the most restrictive, and people can only see your information if you have agreed they can be a friend. 'Friends of friends' can start to spread that information quite a long way, and, of course, 'Everyone' is the widest circulation possible.

The default setting varies from site to site, and you should not assume that the site starts off with the most secure setting.

One of the areas that the media has focused on recently has been the way in which people get tagged in pictures. You can be tagged in a picture someone else has taken and put in their space. You will be told that you have been tagged, and you will have to go and remove the link if you do not want it there. Usually pictures are posted so that friends of friends can see them, and it is in this way that they can be seen by quite a wide audience.

Your password and access

One of the most common ways for privacy to be compromised in social networking happens when you leave the application running on your computer so remember to log off. This is usually found in the top right hand corner of the screen and is either called Log out, or Sign Out. This is particularly an issue for youngsters in school or library situations. It is safest to get into the habit of logging out of the program when you leave your computer, so that no one can pretend to be you and add in information that you were not expecting.

It is also important to guard your user name and password effectively. If someone knows them, they can log in as you and leave inappropriate messages or change things that you did not want to change.

Information to your email

Many of the sites send information to your email inbox, telling you when other people have used the site and left you a message, or asked to be your friend. When this happens you can link back to the social network from the email, but you will still be asked to log in.

Sometimes there are emails that invite you to change your log in or password details. These are not official emails, and, like many others that come from banks and other institutions, are part of the spam created in the system. If any of the emails that come from social networking sites have attachments that invite you to open them or ask you to change your password, or give them some specific data, then they are most unlikely to be real. This is called 'phishing' and it pays to be very cautious and not respond to these emails, and certainly to not open their attachments.

Don't forget

Anyone can pretend to be you if you leave the account open on a communal computer. Make sure you log out.

Finding people you know

A major motivation for joining a particular social network is to find people you already know. Most networks make this as easy as possible for you. They allow you to use your email address book as a source for contacts.

Beware

Make sure you only invite the people you really want to see your pages. Check through the list carefully.

Once the list is provided, you will want to think carefully about each person – you might not want to invite tradesmen or other service providers to be your friend!

The process is generally very efficient and harvests potential friends very quickly. The site then usually provides a way for you to create a message that can go to your contacts, telling them that you would like to connect to them using the social network. They can then reply and accept your invitation or reject it.

An alternative process is to search for people individually. All sites have some search facility available. Sometimes sites ask you to have an alias rather than your real name, and it can sometimes be a little harder to find people that way. Searching in this way can be a lot slower, of course, but adding only one or two people to your network at a time can make it easier to get into the process and to develop an understanding of how the site works.

Netiquette

Some sites have their own set of guidelines or rules for behavior, so that communication between people remains friendly and safe. So this page lists some of the things that are 'etiquette' for the 'net', hence netiquette.

- When you read something on a site that you completely disagree with, make sure your comments are about the point that is being made, and not suggesting that the writer is stupid

- All sites are concerned about racist remarks, comments likely to cause offence to any religious community, or which are pornographic. Don't post anything that could be considered to be any of the above

- Putting your comments in CAPITAL LETTERS to make sure people notice them is considered shouting and should not be done

- It's very important not to break copyright laws. Just because you can copy things easily from Internet sites does not mean you are allowed to. Sites where music, photographs or videos are stored are very concerned about this rule

- You can quote from other people – but do give them credit for the good things they say by naming them in your posting

- Be sensitive to the perspectives of others. Going to a site that supports a particular type of music or a particular band and then saying that band is rubbish is not going to be positively received

- When you are adding a comment to a topic, a video or a piece of writing, make sure your comment is relevant and not going off on a tangent.

- Before you change the subject and talk about something else, make sure there is not a current discussion already up and running

- Don't advertize unless its specifically allowed

Don't forget

Written words can be misinterpreted – especially sarcastic comments.

Beware

Flaming is not allowed – it's the term for aggressive and hostile behaviour between Internet users.

Hot tip

If you are not sure if you have the copyright to something, assume you do not, and either do not use it, or make sure you credit the person you got it from.

Using forums

Before you do anything to contribute to a forum, it is worth spending a bit of time reading what other people have posted. Some forums are 'moderated', which means that someone from the organization takes ownership of them, and checks that there is no offensive materials displayed. The following is a posting from Sam, who moderates a forum on Saga Zone. It gives some sensible forum rules.

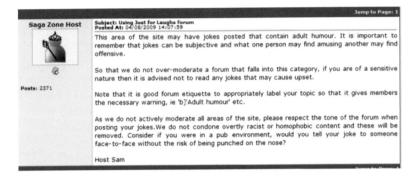

The other real issue with forums is keeping to the subject. You can see from this diagram that there is a great wealth of forums on offer on this site. It is good practice to keep to the subject the forum is debating, and not go off on a tangent.

Depending on the level of activity of a forum, it can be a great way of finding out what other people have experienced, and for tapping into a variety of wisdom and understanding that you might not find in day-to-day life, especially if you have an unusual interest or hobby.

Communities with a purpose

Social networking sites have become a tool used by political organizations to contact and to influence us to vote in particular ways. They are also ways in which private individuals can run campaigns too.

There are two different ways these networks operate. Either the political debate is run within a social networking site – Facebook or MySpace, for example, or a lobbying site is set up and communicates with people through email and links that subscribers can use to send a particular message to the government or other agencies.

Beware

Make sure you know something about the person running a campaigning site. They might not all be as benign as they might seem at first.

This is a page on Facebook that has been created by a Facebook user and to which he has invited others to join to discuss the issues of electoral reform. Some of these pages have hundreds of thousands of viewers with active comments and shared messages.

Don't forget

Some organizations put a lot of effort into running campaigning sites and might ask you for money, as well as email support.

Students for Barack Obama

Weekly Address: The Republican Corporate Power Grab President Obama explains how the most dire warnings about the Citizens United case are being proven valid, even as Republicans in Congress have blocked legislation to fix it: Back in January, in my State of the Union Address, I warned of the danger posed by a Supreme Court ruling called Citizens...

23 hours ago · Share

👍 109 people like this.

💬 View all 89 comments

...cont'd

The other sort of social network site for political purposes is usually run by a lobbying organization, or a charity with a clear purpose and aim. They run campaigns using email and websites and encourage users to communicate with politicians and officials to make changes to the law or to influence you in some other way.

These organizations have their own sites, but use the online facilities to influence citizens across the country.

⊕ CAMPAIGN

SECRET LOBBYING: WE NEED NEW RULES

The government has now announced plans to introduce a **register of lobbyists**. This is great news but lobbyists have vowed to fight it.

Let's make sure the government **holds their nerve** and brings in the new law quickly

EMAIL CAMERON AND CLEGG NOW

MOVEON.ORG
POLITICAL ACTION
Fight Washington Corruption

We need to elect candidates who will make democracy work again for the Other 98% of us—who can't afford to buy elections and hire lobbyists.

Sign the pledge »

MOVEON.ORG
POLITICAL ACTION
Six Weeks to Win parties!

Kick off the election season at Six Weeks to Win parties on Tuesday. We're mobilizing MoveOn members to stop Republicans and their corporate allies from taking over Congress.

Click here to attend a party near you »

These two examples of lobbying forums and sites make it clear how important these websites are. They are not just the province of the young but also have a lot to offer all of us by being engaged in our society.

The next chapter will explore Facebook, perhaps the widest spread social networking site around the world at the moment.

4 Facebook and MySpace

This chapter explores the details of the service offered by Facebook and MySpace, and also shows you how to use these social networking sites effectively.

Creating your account

Signing up for Facebook is a very straightforward affair. Go to www.Facebook.com, complete the information on this form, and then select Sign Up.

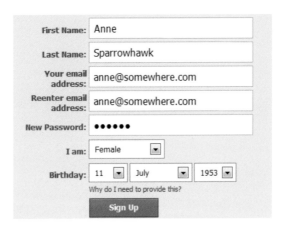

First Name:	Anne
Last Name:	Sparrowhawk
Your email address:	anne@somewhere.com
Reenter email address:	anne@somewhere.com
New Password:	••••••
I am:	Female
Birthday:	11 July 1953

Why do I need to provide this?

Sign Up

Next, type the security check words into the box provided. Sometimes they are very hard to read; click on Try different words to get another set. Alternatively you can listen to the words spelled out against a confusing audio background.

Security check

Enter **both words** below, **separated by a space**.
Can't read the words below? Try different words or an audio CAPTCHA.

issuance towering

Text in the box:

◄ Back   **Sign Up**

By clicking Sign Up, you are indicating that you have read and agree to the Terms of Use and Privacy Policy.

Hot tip

Make sure you've put the space inbetween the two words it has asked for.

Facebook automatically tries to identify existing members that you may already know. You are invited to add these as a friend or to ignore them. If you choose to Add as Friend, a friend request will be sent off to the person in question and they have to approve you as a friend - it's a reciprocal arrangement. This may happen very quickly if they are

...cont'd

actively online, or it could take a little while. Select as many people as you want from this list, or skip to move on to the next step.

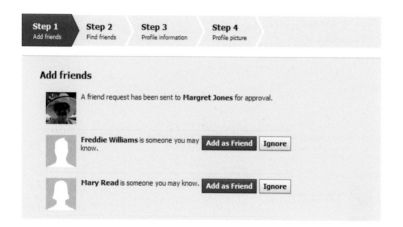

As the next step, Facebook offers you the opportunity to allow it to search your email address book. It can only access emails that are stored on the Internet. If your email is one that it cannot search, it will tell you.

Friends who are already on Facebook will already understand what an invitation to become a friend might mean. For non-Facebook users, a little more information is provided by the system, along with the personal invitation from yourself. The steps in the process are shown on the following page. There is no requirement to invite new users to Facebook, and you can come back to do that later if you wish.

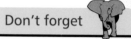

Don't forget

You can start off with just a few friends, to explore Facebook, and then add more friends over time.

Hot tip

Start by inviting people who you contact regularly to be friends. Add less regular contacts after you have used Facebook for a while.

...cont'd

Don't forget

Don't be too nervous about inviting someone to be your friend. They can always ignore your invitation, and that is not considered rude on Facebook.

Allow Facebook to access your email address.

Choose people you want to add as friends.

Be selective in who you invite to join Facebook.

Facebook invitations to your plumber and business contacts might not be appropriate, so be careful of who receives a Facebook invitation at your request. You can also check Select None and move on to the next section.

Creating your profile

You can give a lot of information about yourself, or be much more selective. The next step in creating your account encourages you to identify a High School you attended, and a University and employer. You can Skip these if you want; if you fill them in, Facebook will use that information to try and find friends that you might know.

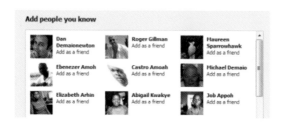

You can choose to add people Facebook offers you as friends, or to Skip this step at this time. Click on the Add as friend text to have a text message sent to the person identified.

Add people you know

Complete the registration process by choosing a photograph of yourself as your profile picture. It can take a picture with your webcam if you have one connected to the computer. Alternatively, you can upload a photograph from your computer. When you have done that, press Save and continue. You will then arrive at your basic home page. Before you can complete any more, you need to go to your email mail box to complete the sign-up process.

...cont'd

Now you have formally joined Facebook, there is more profile information that you can provide. It is gathered through a series of simple forms. Fill in the information you wish to share.

Hot tip

There's a progress bar under your profile picture, which shows how much of your profile you have completed.

1 This menu controls the different sections of the profile

2 The Basic Information is the most important. It is presented as a series of text boxes into which you enter your data

3 You can choose not to have your year of birth included, or your gender. Any sections that you choose not to fill in will not appear on your profile page. You can come back and add more information when you wish, or after you've had more experience in using the site. Make sure you save changes at the bottom of the page

4 You might already have set the profile picture. If not, you can change it from the Profile picture menu.

5 Relationships offers you the opportunity to list family members as well as asking what your relationship status is. This is an area of Facebook that many people take very seriously and relationships have broken up because of the way the situation is described here

Don't forget

You can limit how much profile information people see by limiting information to friends only, but if you don't want to answer the questions, you don't have to.

6 The 'Likes and interests' section records the subjects and activities that you like doing. As you start to fill in the options, a drop down menu will offer you the text. Choose from the text offered or add your own

Hot tip

This Like information will increase as you use the site and choose Like underneath content on the site.

7 The 'Education and work' information has been filled out already, but you can add to it if you wish

57

...cont'd

8 The final section is for contact information - phone, services like Skype, address, and website links. It can be really useful to friends if you have this information here – BUT you need to be really sure that you have the security settings right so that not everyone can see it. We'll come on to that in a moment. Make sure you Save Changes when you have finished

9 Check to see how your profile looks. There might be information presented that you will not want everyone to see. Select Account from the top menu bar and click on Privacy Settings, to set who will see different elements of your information

Privacy Settings

Facebook probably has more discussions in the press about security than most of the other networking sites. This is not because it is less secure than others, but because people have generally been careless about applying the settings that it offers.

If you have friends or family who have not got the settings right, do let them know and encourage them to be more careful. Some of the stories about youngsters finding that their party has been gate-crashed by unwanted guests are true. This has happened because they have posted an invitation to an event that they thought was going just to their friends, but that was not the case.

Choose your privacy settings

Basic directory information
To help real-world friends find you, some basic information is open to everyone. We also suggest setting basics like hometown and interests to everyone so friends can use those to connect with you. View settings

Sharing on Facebook

		Everyone	Friends of friends	Friends only
Everyone	My status, photos, and posts	•		
Friends of friends	Bio and favorite quotations	•		
Friends only	Family and relationships	•		
	Photos and videos I'm tagged in		•	
	Religious and political views		•	
Recommended ✔	Birthday		•	
	Can comment on posts			•
	Places I check in to [?]			•
	Contact information			•
	☑ Let friends of people tagged in my posts see them.			
	✎ Customise settings		✔ This is your current setting.	

You can think of the security as being three growing circles of contacts. Friends only share your most personal details. Friends of friends is a wider network, and Everyone is the whole network of people. Clearly there is little point being on a social networking site if you don't share some information, but you might want to think carefully about whether you want to share your personal life with work colleagues, for example. Teachers have a particular issue, making sure that students don't read about their friend's party, and, perhaps more importantly, don't see the pictures that were taken that night.

Don't forget

Your name, profile picture, gender, current city and friends list are considered public information and available to everyone.

Hot tip

Set the security that applications and settings can access. This is a control on the bottom left of the privacy setting page.

...cont'd

Customizing your settings

This is a straightforward process, so it is one that you can revisit after you have been using Facebook for a while. There are settings that apply to what you put up on the site - these are covered by the 'Things I share' element of the customizable settings. Then there are settings that apply to what you will allow others to send you or share with you. These are covered by the 'Things others share' settings. At any time, you can preview how your Profile will look by selecting View Profile. This bar will be added to your profile page, and you can then return to customize settings further.

This is how your Profile looks to most people on Facebook

Preview how your Profile appears to a specific person: Start typing a friend's name   ‹ Back to Privacy settings

1 Select this button from the privacy settings page

2 You can change any of the elements of information to the level that suits you. Select Customize to set for specific shared friends

3 Select each item from the different sections that you want to change

4 Photos are an area that many people worry about. You can edit the privacy for albums you post, and also for images that other people share.

Edit album privacy for existing photos.

Things others share   Photos and videos I'm tagged in   🔒 Friends of friends ▾

Finding friends and family

During the login process you will have been offered opportunities to use the technology to find family and friends. You can click on any of the links it offers you from your profile entry information. This may find a range of people who you can invite to be your friends.

Facebook can also import the names of people you contact when you use an instant messenger feature from a site - Skype perhaps. You have to provide your contact name and password in order to give Facebook permission to do the search. The site does not record the password.

If you do not have many electronic contacts with people, then these searches might not produce many contacts. You might also want to restrict yourself to contacting just a few people using Facebook.

You can search for a specific person by typing their name into the search box. A list of potential people will come up on screen, with their profile photograph and a link to their profile. Even if it's someone you have not seen for a while, it should be enough to identify them. If you are not sure you have the right person, or it's been a really long time since you contacted them, you can use the Send a Message button to send them a message without asking them to become a friend. Alternatively, select Add as Friend. You can then choose to send a message, together with the friend request.

Hot tip

Use the Send a Message button to contact people who you are not certain you know.

...cont'd

Hot tip

Choose from friends of friends carefully. It's quite easy to add people later.

When you have sent your request, Facebook will offer a set of pictures and links to people that your new friend already knows, and who it thinks you might know too. You can then choose to add those people to your friends list.

Another way of widening your network is to look at their friends link. Through this, you can find other people that you know and invite them to become friends too.

Receiving friend requests

As you start to use Facebook, you'll find that people start to find you too. You will receive Friend requests in the email account you used when you joined Facebook. You can choose to accept them and they will then become a friend, or you can ignore them and there will be no further action.

Groups

Facebook has had a reputation for getting groups together for all sorts of current affairs activities - who is voting in the election, should we be fighting in Afghanistan, cutting bankers' bonuses, and so on. It's very easy to join a group, and to start one too.

1 Select Groups from the Applications submenu in the left menu.

2 Select Friend's groups to see a list that you might want to join. If you do, simply click Join

3 To create your own group, select Create Group, fill in the information on the form and complete the security information, making it an open or closed group if you wish

4 You can then invite friends to join by selecting Friends from a picture box. You can also create an advert to encourage people to join, which Facebook will then place on appropriate users' home pages

Mandolinists forever

A group to encourage mandolin playing

Anne Sparrowhawk likes this advert.

👍 Like

News, views, and applications

News

Once you have gained some friends on Facebook, you'll start getting News from them. Some of the messages will be messages just to you – see the message from Jonathan to me in the following illustration. Others will be messages posted on a friend's 'wall' and which can be read by anyone visiting. They appear in your News Feed, so that you can keep up to date with what they are doing or thinking.

Hot tip

Click Edit Options at the bottom of the News Feed to stop news from particular friends appearing here. It will shorten your News Feed list.

You can comment on the posting by selecting Comment. A box opens for you to write in. That is then given as a message directly to the author of the posting. Other people can see it on your Wall and write a comment back.

'See Wall-to-Wall' is a useful feature that enables you to read the communications you have had with another person over time.

In this case, the content sequence starts at the top of the page and the new entries are joined at the bottom.

'Like' connects you to a Page. The page will be linked to your profile and you will be displayed on that page too. When you want to go to a space to start a conversation going for yourself, click on your name and go to your wall.

Your wall

As well as responding to friends and family, you will probably want to share some information yourself. The place you do this is your Wall. It records a sequence of activity that you have been involved in, starting with the most recent at the top.

You might have looked at other people's walls by now and will have seen that the information or comments they post do not have to be very long or very profound. In fact, for many youngsters, it's a record of where they are and who they're with as well as how they feel about what is going on!

To publish a comment, just click in the comment box and write what you want. You can attach photos, videos, information about an event or a web link to your posting. You can now also decide who the specific comment goes to. This is a new feature of Facebook, and it allows you to decide the privacy for each posting. When you are happy that you have said what you want, and to whom, click Share.

Hot tip

If you don't want to send someone a message, but just remind them you are there, you can Poke them. Poke can be found underneath your friend's profile picture.

Attaching further information to the posting is very easy, Find the file on your computer and then click upload, or, alternatively, you can take a picture with a webcam.

At the bottom of your wall there is a section that lists the Recent Activity. This can act as a route to either find other friends or join groups with shared interests. For example, one of my activities is playing the mandolin. Linking from 'My activities' in the recent activity list, you can go to a

Hot tip

If you want to add a selection of pictures, you would be better off creating an album first.

...cont'd

community page about Playing the Mandolin. Here you might be able to find other people who list that as an activity and contact them, or, as in this case, find an event that you might want to go to focusing on your hobby.

From time to time, you or friends might post things on your wall that you feel are no longer relevant or is inappropriate. You can easily remove them by clicking on the Remove button that appears when you move your mouse over the relevant part of the screen.

Applications

Facebook offers a number of applications that are built in to support you writing comments - photos, video and links, for example. There are several others that are worth exploring in a bit more detail.

- Events - Facebook allows you to plan and share an event, and to encourage people to come to it

- Photo albums help you manage sets of photos

- Chat allows you to chat online to a friend

- Groups can be set up to foster an interest or support a sport or music group

Events

1 Add the Events tab by selecting + and clicking on Events

2 Click on Create an event to open the template to give details of time and location

3 You can select potential guests from Facebook by clicking the Select guests button. This offers a list of friends who you could specifically invite. Choose them and Save and close the dialog window

4 Make sure you only select the Anyone can view button if it is a public event. It is useful to have the guest list on the event page, so others can see invitees

...cont'd

Photos - yours and others

1 Select the Photos tab from the navigation bar

2 Select the button to the right to create your album

3 Give the album a name and location. Set the privacy setting to an appropriate level. You can also make it available to specific, named people

4 The next step is to identify photos on your computer and choose them - the Select Photos button. When you have selected all you want, press the Upload button and you will see a progress bar to indicate how it is going

5 Give each photo a caption. Click the + sign over the face of any person in the photo. Choose the name from a list of your friends or add one

6 If someone has tagged you in a picture in their album, you will find out about it in your News Feed

7 Find the picture where you have been tagged. If you're not happy with this, click the Remove tag under the photo

8 To make sure you know that a photograph has been posted and tagged with your name, visit the Account Menu and open Account Settings. The third tab is Notifications. Click on this to review the notifications you will receive when people communicate with you on Facebook

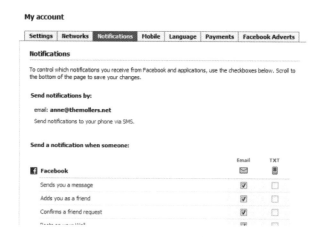

...cont'd

Chat

The Chat window is always available when you are logged into Facebook, and it allows you to have a conversation with a friend who is also logged onto Facebook. The conversation is just between the two of you.

1 Click on this box at the bottom right of your screen

2 Click on it to open the list of people you know who are online now

3 Select one of those names and a window will open in which your conversation will appear. Type a message and press Return. Your message will appear with 'Me' above it and a time. As your friend responds, the conversation will develop in that window

4 The conversation will be retained for a while, but not permanently

5 Creating a number of Friends Lists is really useful here. Click on Friend Lists and type a name in to create one

6 Select Edit next to the name you've typed in, and a box with your friends in will appear. Select the people you want and 'Save list' when you've chosen

Playing games

There are many games available through Facebook. Lots of them can be played enjoyably alone. However, the reason a lot of games are posted here is to allow their players to be competitive, and to challenge your friends and family to see who can gain the highest scores.

1. Select Games from the menu on the left of the home screen

2. There are a list of games on the right of the screen. Choose one of them to try it out

3. Click Allow on the request for permission for the game company to access your personal details, so that you can be linked to others, or compared with your friends

4. The format of the games varies enormously. You will, at some point, be asked to invite friends to play as well. If you do, then the leader board of the game is sometimes set up to record and compare your scores with just those of your friends. Until you have friends to compare with, the scores may be more general

...cont'd

5 A link from within the game will offer you a picture box to choose your friends you want to challenge to play the game

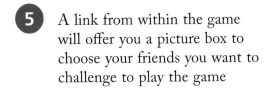

6 This creates an invitation that you can preview before you send it to your chosen friends. When you've sent it within Facebook, you will also be asked if you'd like to send emails to people from your email contacts

7 Friends may share their scores at games with you, to encourage you to play the games they like

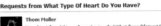

8 Quizzes are a popular activity too, and are often shared among users

9 While you wait to have your quiz scored, you are invited to send the same quiz to up to 6 friends

Your MySpace account

Many of the features and activities that have been described about Facebook are also to be found in MySpace. This section will outline some of the practicalities of setting up a MySpace account, but will also explore some of the special features MySpace offers. Whether you have both a Facebook and a MySpace account will depend on who you want to communicate with, and which network they have joined. Go to www.myspace.com to join.

Signing up

This follows a similar process to Facebook, storing your email address, password, name, gender and age. There are separate log ins for Musicians, Comedians and Filmmakers, with clear information about copyright and what can and cannot be posted legally. Once you have signed up, an email will be sent to the mailbox you signed up with. Select 'Confirm your MySpace account' to open your MySpace account.

Hi, Anne!

Thanks for joining MySpace!

Confirm your MySpace account

Here's your account info for logging in:

Facebook and MySpace share many similar processes in uploading photographs and information. Click on the blue camera icon to upload a photo for your profile. MySpace allows you to personalize your profile and make it look different from others in ways that Facebook does not.

Personalizing your profile

Select Profile from the top menu bar and then New Profile Guide. This will present you with a number of useful videos that outline the process you can follow to create a profile page that reflects you in terms of color, layout and motif.

Beware

MySpace is currently operating a Beta version of the Profile. This may change as the product goes live. The principles are sure to stay the same.

Themes

1 First you are offered themes to choose from. The Preview button allows you to preview what it will look like

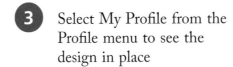

2 If you decide you want to keep it, select this button at the top of the screen

3 Select My Profile from the Profile menu to see the design in place

Beware

The menu options from Music and, further to the right, access the general MySpace pages, not materials specific to you. Your own music can be accessed from the Music menu underneath the word Stream.

Click on terms in the menu bar on the left to see different pages of your content in the chosen design.

...cont'd

To edit your profile and add more information than you had to provide when you set up the account, you need to do the following.

1 Select Edit Profile from the top of the menu on your stream

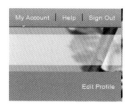

2 You can then access a menu that allows you to add specific information about your interest, schooling and the companies you have worked for

3 The Basic information will be mostly complete. You can set a Display Name there. You'll see that a lot of people on MySpace use that to add a nickname – Saucy Sam, for example

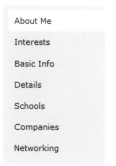

4 The Details section adds information that could be useful if you are looking for a relationship with someone. It includes a range of information you can choose to include if you wish. When you've updated the information, make sure you save changes.

Don't forget

You can set the information about school to include the years when you were at the institution. It has a list of schools, which includes Universities too.

Beware

Do not give information here that you really only want to share with friends.

...cont'd

Photos

 1 Select Photos from the menu under your profile image and select Upload Photos

2 Find the photos on your computer and select them. A progress bar shows how the upload is going

3 When they have uploaded, images have a caption slot and a tool to provide a tag.

4 Save the data and view the images on your Stream or in the photos section

Music

1 Create your playlist by selecting the Music menu from the top menu bar. This offers access to all sorts of music and opens an additional row of menu items

2 Select My Music in the lower menu and on the left you'll find My Profile Playlist

3 Drag songs here to add to your playlist on your profile

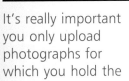

Beware

It's really important you only upload photographs for which you hold the copyright.

Hot tip

Musicians can upload their original music to MySpace for you to listen to for free. They like to get feedback on their songs.

Movies

This section provides articles and other information about movies, celebrities and television. Select this button on anything you want to follow. A link will be placed on your Stream and you will be updated when there is news.

Video

This section provides video content made by professionals and also other MySpace users. You can upload your own videos, providing you are the copyright owner. You can comment on the work of others too.

Games and Applications

As with Facebook, MySpace offers a vast number of games and applications that need to be loaded. You will be asked to give permission for the game to access your data, so that it can personalize your experience and give you competitive scores against your friends or other players.

Events

You can use MySpace to advertize an event, but this section is also very much used by professional companies advertizing gigs and concerts. You can search for events by location and type – festivals, art, sport, etc. You can create a quick event, which works well for arrangements for a small group of friends meeting for a meal, for example.

Don't forget

You will find the Apps you have loaded under the More menu item in your Stream.

Beware

If you do use MySpace to create an event, make sure you remember to set the guest list carefully, so that you don't have unwanted guests.

Family, friends and privacy

As well as using your email contacts to find potential friends, and searching for a specific name, MySpace also offers a browse facility that offers two alternative ways of finding potential friends. One shows people who are currently online. You are invited to chat with them through the chat link button next to their picture.

The other allows you to specify what sort of person you are looking for, taking information from their profile, including relationship status, age, ethnicity, smoker, and so on. The results of this search are displayed in the same way as the 'online at the moment' list.

My Visitors setting leaves a record of other people's sites that you visit, and indicates who has visited your pages too. Both you and the site you're visiting have to have the facility turned on for it to work.

The privacy settings in MySpace allow the site to use your name and photo to indicate that you are a trendsetter. MySpace logs who visits particular music or video content. When other people visit that track or video, they might see the names and profile pictures of other people who have already looked at it – trendsetters. If you do not want to be tagged in this way, you will need to deselect the Trendsetter option.

Beware

It's easy to chat with someone straight away by clicking on the Online Now icon – but you might want to check out their profile first.

Beware

Leaving a record of where you have been can be great – BUT, if you visit sites and wish you hadn't, then that site will also know that you have been there and can contact you again.

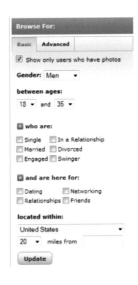

5 Using Skype to Talk

This chapter explains how to set up a Skype account, and how to use it to talk to friends anywhere.

What you need to Skype

Skype is an online telephone service that allows you to talk to other Skype users anywhere in the world for free. You can also call people who only have a regular telephone line, if you don't mind paying a little for that service. Skype-to-Skype calls can also be made to several people at once, so you can connect a group of friends or family together too and share in a discussion.

To make this all happen you need the following:

- A computer connected to the Internet and the use of a web browser

- A download of the Skype software installed on the computer

- Speakers and a microphone to hear and talk through. While many laptop computers offer these as built-in functions, to enjoy really good quality conversations you will probably prefer to have a headset with a boom microphone.

- Most people also have a webcam (a camera connected to your computer that sends video images via the Internet). This is not essential, but adds a lot to the interactive experience.

Download the software

1 Go to the Skype website – www.skype.com. This page offers marketing information about Skype paid-for services. The service is free if you only want to talk to other Skype users

2 The top menu bar offers a Get Skype option and you should select this

Get Skype

3 This will lead to a screen from which you can select the right version of Skype for your computer

Hot tip

If you think you might talk online a lot, it's a good idea to get a comfortable headset, including microphone.

80

On your computer

Install Skype, add your friends as contacts, then call, video call and instant message with them for free. Call people who aren't on Skype too, at really low rates.

4 When you have checked that it is offering you the right version, select this button

5 The dialog box will ask you to save this file, and, depending on your browser, you will need to confirm that you want to install the program

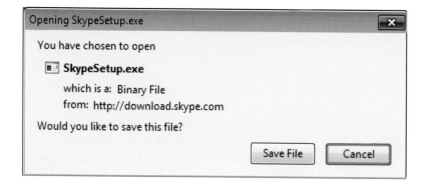

6 Two more dialog boxes invite you to confirm that you want to download the files and also to choose English as your language

7 When it has completed, click on Finish

Hot tip

Using a browser that is fairly up-to-date will help make Skype run more efficiently. If you've avoided downloading the latest version of the browser, now might be the time to do it!

Create your Skype account

1 Fill in the fields to create your new account. Choose a user name that will mean something to the people you know. Write down the Full name and Password somewhere where you will be able to find them again.

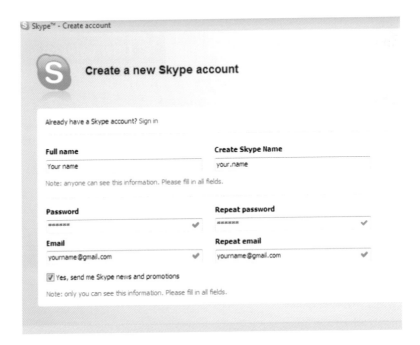

2 Open your account using the button shown

I agree - create account

3 Sometimes the Skype name you want is not available. You will then be given a variety of names to choose from

4 Choose a name, and then Create your account

Create account

Your Skype profile

Setting up your Skype profile can be as limited and simple as confirming the country you live in and adding a city. The purpose of this is to make sure that people choose the right person to talk to. There are, of course, people with the same name, but linking that name to a location will reduce the confusion. This information is public - everyone using Skype can see it.

You are also invited to put in the date of your birthday. Entering this information helps people to speak to the right person. If you are John Doe from Atlanta, but clearly not 57, then that will encourage someone trying to call you to find the person they really want to speak to. If you do enter your birthdate, your friends will get a reminder when it's your birthday.

Don't forget

You can also ask people for their Skype name, rather than having to find it in the directory.

You are invited to give your cellphone number as well. This can only be seen by your contacts. This can be very useful if you are offline they will have another way of finding you.

Once you have entered this information, click OK and you will have created your basic profile on Skype.

...cont'd

There are other elements of the Profile that you can add.

1 To do that, you need to login to the program from this button, or from your program menu

2 This will open the basic Skype screen, which will have your Skype contact name at the top

3 Select Personalize to open the Profile menu

4 Choose Edit Your Profile. This opens a screen where you can make changes to the information you have previously entered, and also add home and office telephone numbers your contacts will be able to see

5 Select Change picture, which gives you the option of choosing a photograph or picture you have stored on your computer, some ready made icons, or to create your own personalized Weemee, as shown here

There are benefits from choosing any of these three options. Your photograph is recognizable by people who know you, but you might feel this provides too much personal information.

6 When you have made your choice, click OK and the image will appear underneath your Skype name.

7 If you want, you can add a video or message that will appear next to your picture, and which only your friends can see. Click on the Change your mood button from the Profile to choose a video or write a message

8 Complete the profile by selecting Update.

9 When you have completed your profile, it is still possible to change it at any time. Simply repeat the process again

So far we have set up the software, and have the Internet working. The next step is to make a space where you can Skype efficiently. You can use a laptop to Skype, but if you are going to Skype regularly, and want to share video images of yourself, then it's worth making some desk space available. Thinking about the lighting is particularly important.

Beware

The video message might be distracting. The message needs to be relevant to anyone who you have in your contacts, not just a few friends.

Hot tip

Skype should be able to find your headphones and microphone as part of the set up process. If you are experiencing difficulty on a PC, try exploring the menu from the volume icon on your Windows toolbar.

Setting up sound and video

Using a pair of headphones with integral microphone improves the quality of the call. Most computers are now color coded, so that you get the phone jacks into the right socket. The convention is that the green jack is for the audio and the pink for the microphone. Some headphones have a volume control on the cable. Make sure that the control is not set to Mute (unless you want to be silent, of course.)

Most webcams come with software that needs to be installed. Usually this is simple to do, by following the instructions provided. Locating the webcam is sometimes more tricky. Attaching it to the top of your monitor is probably the best place for it – you can still operate the computer and, to some extent, forget about it. You need to make sure it can be tilted at the right angle to see you in front of it. Some have an inbuilt microphone. If you are using a headset, then make sure the webcam's microphone is turned off.

You might want to adjust the light source in your room. Overhead or back lights make for very dark screens. Placing a table lamp as shown here improves the quality of video images considerably.

Beware

Make sure any inbuilt webcam is turned off, if you are adding an external one.

Webcam - Angle this to suit

Lamp - Angled to light you from the side

Microphone Headset

...cont'd

Use the test service
Skype provides an Echo / Sound Test Service - you'll find it on your contacts list.

1 Click on the listing

2 To the right of the screen, choose Check Settings

3 Check that your system is working correctly. The microphone is on Mute in this set up

Hot tip

You might need to adjust the sound using the icons on your taskbar. A microphone with a red cross over it will show you the microphone control is set to mute.

4 When all is in place, select Call. Listen to the message, and then record your own

5 Make any adjustments you need to volume of sound, either in what you hear or your own voice.

Sharing account details

So now you have an account, your computer is all set up, but how do you find people to talk to, and let them know you are on Skype?

There are several different ways of doing this, and you will probably use a combination of these to make the service work.

If there is a particular person you want to contact, click on the directory and it will open up a screen into which you can type the name of the person, their Skype name, or their email address.

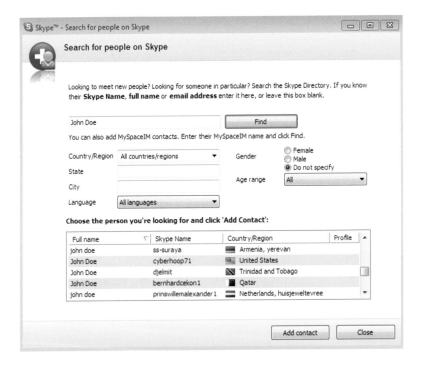

You can make the search more specific by entering country, gender or age restrictions. Without these restrictions, this general search will provide the list of all the people called John Doe who are registered on Skype. When you have found the person you are looking for, click on Add contact, and that person's Skype details will be added to your contact list.

...cont'd

A different approach is to use lists of contacts that you already have in your email address book, or through Facebook or a range of other services.

1 From the main menu, choose Contacts, and then Import Contacts

Who's on Skype? Check your address books.

Pick the one(s) you use.

Facebook   Hotmail   Gmail   Other ▾

Beware

There may be people in your address list that you don't want to talk with on Skype. Look through the list of people it offers you carefully.

2 Select from the buttons here, using the Other button to choose Outlook or one of the other services

Import your Gmail address book

Gmail username

Gmail password

Please only give us your user name and password if you are authorised to allow us to access your contacts on your behalf.

Import   Cancel

🔒 Skype doesn't keep your login details.

3 Enter the username and password for your email service and select Import. Skype will then search through your list of email addresses and identify those that have a Skype address.

...cont'd

4 When it has completed its search, it will present you with the list of people from your address book that it knows

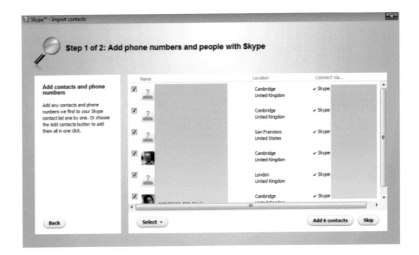

5 Use the ticks to the left of the image and name (they are obscured here to protect my contacts details) and then click on Add Contacts to add them to your Skype address list

6 As Skype completes that process, it sends a message to your contacts to tell them that you have joined Skype and have asked to share your details

7 Skype produces a list of people from your mailbox who are not yet on Skype. It produces this message, which you can choose to send to these contacts. Choosing Skip will mean that no one is emailed

8 When you have identified the contacts that you want to keep, they will be added to your Skype Contacts list.

9 You can tell if the contact is online or not by the color of the symbol next to the Skype name. A green symbol with a white tick means they are online and available for a call

Other useful software

1 Open the Tools menu for its Extras section, which offers Pamela Call Recorder

2 Choose the green button and follow the instructions for the download options.

3 Allow access to Skype for the recorder in order to initialize it, ready for any call you want to record

Your invitation email

Your name

Your name

Your email address

yourname@gmail.com

Message

Hi! Just dropping you a quick note to let you know I'm on Skype. If you download it too, we can call, video call and instant message each other free - even if we're on opposite sides of the world. Plus, it's free to download. Get it and add me as a contact! My Skype Name is your.name12.

Send email   Skip

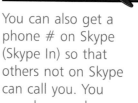

Hot tip

You can also get a phone # on Skype (Skype In) so that others not on Skype can call you. You can choose where this number appears, so that people who phone you often without Skype only need to pay for a local call.

Hot tip

This can be a great way of sharing your Skype call with other family members who couldn't be there at the time.

Making a call

Hot tip

When you start Skype, you can see who has tried to contact you and when.

Beware

Skype is free and offers a great facility. It is not a guaranteed service, though, so if the call is really important make sure you have a backup plan in case the connectivity is not good.

This is the information that is available when you select one of your contacts to make a call. The first thing you need to notice is that, in addition to the name of the person you are calling and their Skype name, it gives their location and time. This can help you avoid embarrassing attempted phone calls in the middle of their night!

Select either of the green buttons to make an audio or video call. The bottom part of the screen monitors the call. The text box at the bottom of the screen allows you to enter text as you are talking. If the connectivity is not good, this can be a useful way of letting the other person know that you cannot see them or hear them, and perhaps suggesting that they turn the video service off. It is useful for adding weblinks and sending them through to the other person too. Click the blue button to send. The interactions with a particular contact are shown on this screen, the most recent at the top.

Multiple call-attendees

It can be really useful to set up calls that include a number of people. You can add people whilst you are on a call, or set up a group call beforehand.

1 Select one of the people you want to call.

2 Click on the Add people button and select the names of the other people from your contacts list that you want to be present

3 Click on the Save group in Contacts button to make this into a group that you can call another time

4 Give it a name to add to your Contact list, which will automatically call up all the group members when the next call is made

Don't forget

You can always add new people to the list when you are ready to make the call.

Taking a call

The ring tone is distinctive, and, as it rings, a window pops up on screen with 'Answer', 'Answer with video' or 'Decline' on it. You can choose to speak with or without video, or you can answer with audio and then add video function in as the call progresses.

There are a few things to remember:

- Video takes up quite a lot of bandwidth, so, if the sound is not good, turn off the video at either or both ends

- If you decide to record the call, it is polite to tell the person you are talking with

- If there's a lot of delay or feedback on the call, it is best for one person to talk uninterupted. The audible agreement that we often make can interfere with the call, as it distracts the speaker. When one person finishes talking then the other can start

- Using the text message feature at the bottom of the screen can be a great way of sharing links and messages if the connectivity is not good

- A group call works best if only one person speaks at a time. Have someone act as chairman

- The features we have talked about in this chapter are all provided on the free service. If you want to be able to phone people who are not on Skype, then you need to upgrade to a paid-for service

Skype makes it possible for people to have conversations when they are the other side of the world. Do remember that the time zones still apply, so be considerate when you make your call.

6 Friends Reunited

This chapter demonstrates how to use Friends Reunited to coordinate activities with groups or friends.

Creating your account

Friends Reunited has been operational since 1999. Initially it was a site that charged for nearly all of its services. Now its services are free to contact old friends and colleagues, and it continues to be the premier site for connecting to school friends, and also for organizing a school reunion.

1 Go to www.friendsreunited.com

2 Fill in the information required on the template

3 Filling in the 'Tell your friends more about yourself' information will be available for anyone to read on the site. You can change it later, though. You can write as much or as little as you like

4 When you have completed the form, click on Register, that will take you to the initial search page. Here you can search for schools, university, armed forces, sports clubs and charities, as well as pubs, workplaces and streets

5 As you fill these in, more options become apparent, moving down from country, to region and town

Don't forget

You can contact people in schools in other countries too.

Don't forget

You don't have to write a full life history here – choosing from the text and information boxes offered is quick and easy to do.

Finding Friends

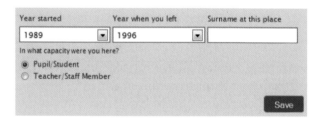

1 Whether you find a school, a place of work or a street, you can then give a little more information about yourself. For example, when you started and left the school, when you lived in the house and what the house number was.

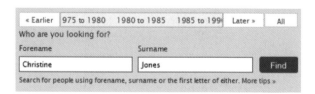

2 Click Save and it will join you to the community for that school

3 Alternatively, you can browse an institution or a location and find the names of people who have joined up based on a certain year

You are now in a position to decide whether or not to contact the person you have found, and get back in touch with them again.

Beware

Try to be as accurate as you can with the dates you give – you can find yourself invited to strange reunions if you get them wrong!

97

Don't forget

You can read the profile of people you have known without having to contact them, or without them knowing their details have been read by you.

Contacting friends

Contact Paul – **it's completely free!**

When you have found someone to communicate with, you can contact them in any of three different ways.

- You can send them a mail, which is personal and will not be seen by other people visiting the site

- You can leave them a comment, which will be seen by anyone who visits their profile. There is a limit of 1000 characters to the comment box

- You can send them a Buzz - choose a graphic and a simple message from the drop down list. Your message is left on your friend's profile, together with your name and a link back to your profile.

When you send the message or post the Buzz, Friends Reunited will send the person you have found an email to tell them that something has been left on their profile, so they are prompted to go and find out about it.

When you are visiting a profile, you are also offered links to people that the site thinks you might know. Selecting More will pull up a list of possible friends.

You can choose to remove them from the list if you either don't know them, or don't want to have contact.

If you select Yes next to the person's name, or Add as friend next to the name in the full list, you will be offered two options of friendship.

If you follow someone in Friends Reunited, they will not get messages to say that you have looked them up.

- Following someone in Friends Reunited is a bit like bookmarking their page. When they update something on their page you will automatically get an update of that on your homepage too

- Friends and Family sets up a link whereby the people you have identified will be asked to accept a Friend Request from you. Your profile photographs, blogs and news is shared with them

If you visit the My Friends option from the Friends menu you will find a list of your friends, you can then change their status appropriately.

You can manage your relationship with each of your friends using the options listed here. If you select Manage, you can remove the friend from your friend list or change them as someone who you want to promote to Friends and Family.

Creating your profile

1 Select My Profile from the Profile menu

2 The profile has taken some information from your initial sign-up data and published it to the profile. Here you can now add information where you choose by selecting the blue text. In many cases, this opens option boxes where you can select appropriate text. You can also add a blog if you wish

3 You can also control who can see the information you have created by selecting Set privacy. If you want to reorder the information on your profile, you can do this too, by selecting 'Move section' and then dragging the element up or down the Profile page

4 You can either upload a photograph of yourself as your profile picture, or create one using WeeMee, using the link at the bottom of the profile page

5 Don't forget to select Save as you complete the different elements of the profile

Adding photos and videos

1 Select My Profile from the Profile menu and choose the Add photos and videos option beneath that. Decide whether the images you want to save relate to a school, organization or create and name a new album. Set the audience and browse your computer to find the images you want

2 The album will be created and you will see how the process is progressing

3 When the photos have uploaded, you can view and add information about them. The tools at the bottom of the picture allow you to rotate the image as well as delete it from your album, if you want

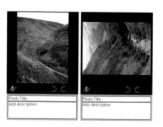

4 You can add tags to the image to show who is in the picture

5 If the person is known to Friends Reunited, a message will be sent to them saying they have been tagged in a picture. If not, there is an opportunity to email them to tell them about it

...cont'd

Other features of photographs

There are some other things to think about with photographs on Friends Reunited.

- Of course, it is only possible to upload digital images. Some of the more interesting photographs may need to be scanned in order to be uploaded. An image can be up to 3Mb, so it should be possible to save an image at a good resolution to see the faces of the people present

- If you really don't want other people to tag you in their pictures, change the setting by going to Privacy Settings and following the link at the bottom of the page

- If you have been tagged by other people in their uploaded pictures, a copy of the picture will be placed in your album page. Go to My photos and videos to see it

- If you have been incorrectly tagged in a picture, you can remove it by clicking on the remove tag text

Uploading videos

This is exactly the same process as adding photographs. Once the video has been uploaded, there is a conversion process that it follows, which takes a few minutes. There is a limit of 10MB for a video file size, so it is worth checking that on your computer before you try to upload it.

Groups, boards and chat

An active part of the site is the group space. There are groups on a very wide range of subjects, each of which has a message board space, like a forum on other sites, and the opportunity to join a live chat.

1 Find a group you might be interested in by choosing the Groups menu

2 Find a group offers a search engine to search all the groups available

3 Browse groups provides a list of categories of groups. This one has 124 different groups within it

4 Specific groups are shown at the next level down, and you can see how many members each group has

5 You can Join the group there, or Browse to see what they are discussing

6 The date is included in the posting, so you can see how recent and active the conversation has been

...cont'd

Posting to a message board

When you find a message board you want to write on, add a new posting at the bottom of the page.

Don't forget

If it's a very active message board, the conversation may have moved on from the first message. Read the last two or three messages before leaving your contribution.

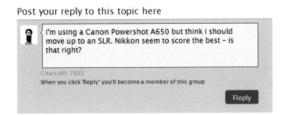

Post your reply to this topic here

I'm using a Canon Powershot A650 but think I should move up to an SLR. Nikon seem to score the best – is that right?

Chars left: 7883

When you click 'Reply' you'll become a member of this group

Reply

When you have completed your posting, and clicked on Reply, the message will appear at the top of the message boards, just under the question that started it all off.

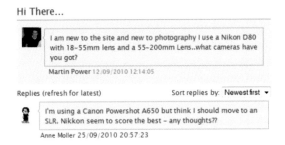

Hi There...

I am new to the site and new to photography I use a Nikon D80 with 18–55mm lens and a 55–200mm Lens..what cameras have you got?

Martin Power 12/09/2010 12:14:05

Replies (refresh for latest)   Sort replies by: Newest first ▼

I'm using a Canon Powershot A650 but think I should move to an SLR. Nikkon seem to score the best – any thoughts??

Anne Moller 25/09/2010 20:57:23

Once you have posted to a message board, you will have joined that particular group. The 'My Groups' list on your Groups menu will itemize the groups you have joined.

Don't forget

You can leave a group if you want by selecting Leave group from the listing in your My Groups menu.

Creating your own topic

1 Search within the message board to make sure you have a new topic. Check out individual words as well as phrases

2 Go to the bottom of the list and complete the Add Topic template. You need to give the topic a meaningful name and then add a message to start the board rolling – a question is a good starting point

...cont'd

Creating your own group

It may be that you will search the Groups and not find a topic that has already been covered. It is worth searching carefully to make sure that is the case, as it is very annoying if a new group gets started that actually covers the interest areas of an existing group.

1 Search or browse for a group, and you will find a menu on the left of the screen that offers you an option to Create a group. Select this.

2 If you plan to set up a group based on a particular location – Oxford reading group, as it shows here, make sure you have selected the 'directory of places' link just above this text box to make sure there is not a regional group already.

3 Give your group a name and then choose a category from the drop down list, and a type from the radio buttons offered

4 Type in the description, of your group in less than 200 characters. Select Create

5 Invite friends to join the group by selecting this button. Choose friends

Invite friends

...cont'd

Chatting

Joining a group chat will make you a member of the group. Some are lively with lots of members online. Familiarity with text-speak will be a bonus and aid communication.

As you can see, you chat with a number of people in the room at once; there can be up to 20 people present. This differs from chat resources offered by other social networking sites. You can select Group Chats - a green button at the bottom right of your screen. This opens up the menu shown here. Choose View all chats taking place now to find an active chat session to join.

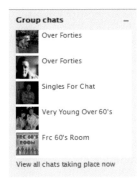

When you join a chat session, it's a good idea to start off by saying hello. Members already chatting will probably greet you back. Similarly, when you are about to leave, it is good practice to say goodbye. Use the other person's name if you are answering a specific comment.

No record is kept of conversations – the text disappears into the ether.

Organizing a reunion

Friends Reunited offer some helpful tools to support you in organizing a reunion. The activity is based around the places or institutions that you belong to., assuming that you will be trying to arrange a reunion of school friends or sports team members, and so on.

1 Go to the school, college or other place that you want to create the reunion for and select the Reunion button

College

Members	Photos and videos	Teachers/staff	Reunions	Message boards

Create a reunion

1 Details ▷ **2 Invitations** ▷ **3 Finished**

Don't worry if you haven't finalised everything, you can edit this section later.

Reunion Title (required)

> Reunion for those of us who started in 1971

Reunion details (required)

> Let's meet in Cambridge and have some time around the weekend, not all following the events planned by the college.

Chars left: 2000

Start date (required)

> 23 Sep 2011

Start time

> 19 ▾ 45 ▾

End date

> 25 Sep 2011

End time

> 23 ▾ 30 ▾

If you don't know the exact date, don't worry, you can comeback and update it at any time.

2 Fill in the event details as you are invited to do so. It is likely that you will initially not have firm times and locations, and might not even be sure of the exact date, but you can still use this form to send something out to gauge interest

3 You can then choose to have the invitation sent out to all the members on the site list who left between specified dates - this could be one year or several, but

Beware

It can be a lot of work to organize a reunion. Make sure you have people to help you do things. Perhaps invite a small group to work on this first before you send out the mass invitations.

Don't forget

Double check the information you send out very carefully before it gets posted on the site.

...cont'd

Hot tip

If you just want to invite people from one school year, put the same year in both the From and To boxes.

the years in question must be sequential – 1982 to 1987. It cannot be 1982-1983 and 1986-1987 – that would have to be done with two separate reunion invitations

4 You can review how many people will be invited, but you cannot 'pick and choose' who will and who will not be on the list

Hot tip

Lots of people are nervous about reunions. Make your message reassuring!

5 Personalize your group invitation so that it excites the recipients. Select Finish and Friends Reunited will send out the invitations within the next 24 hours.

6 A message board can also be used to discuss the event further, and to manage communication between the attendees and yourself, as coordinator

7 Saga Zone

Saga Zone is really a portal, and this chapter explores its facilities, both for members only and those open to a wider readership

Creating your account

Saga Zone is the social networking area that is related to the Saga Magazine portal. It is restricted to those over 50 years of age, but anyone over that age can join.

1 Go to www.sagazone.co.uk

2 Select this button to access the online form

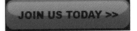

3 Complete the form, with your name and email, and choose a password. Click register

4 You will then be sent an email with a pin number, for you to use when you log into the site for the first time

Verify Email

An email was sent from us containing a 5 digit 'Pin Number'. Please e

Activation Code:

Saga Zone content

Saga Zone News is the home page for Saga Zone and is generally produced by the staff who manage the site. It also has links to other sections of the site. There are two different ways of navigating - the big blue buttons and the menus accessed from the tool bar above.

In general, the blue buttons are the easiest ways of finding your way around the site. Each links through to a section of the site with a specific type of material - forums, photographs, blogs, and so on. Before you explore that in detail, you should update your profile. The best way of updating your profile is through About Me.

Don't forget

You can always look at the magazine content to get some inspiration for your contribution to Saga Zone.

...cont'd

Your Saga Zone profile

How much information you choose to give about yourself is entirely up to you. The more you provide, the more likely you are to find like-minded people to communicate with.

1 Choose Edit My Profile from the About Me menu

2 At the bottom of the screen is an area where you can write 'About Me'

3 You can add some background information

> **About Me**
>
> **Interests**
>
> **Background**
> Educationalist have been involved in a number of different types of project, researching ICT and education

4 It will appear like this on screen. There are a number of prepared headings you can use to give information. Choose only those you feel apply to you

Areas of Expertise
Once took a degree in philosophy. Didn't do me much good, there's no demand for professional philosophers, so I remained poor.

Books
Avid reader, anything from Dickens to A S Byatt

Dislikes
prudes, snobs, bullies

Music
yes!

Hot tip

If you don't have a real interest in one of the sections of the profile you are offered, just leave it out.

Beware

Don't write information here that you wouldn't want everyone to read. You don't have to have your age in your profile, if you'd rather not.

...cont'd

5 Select Edit My Avatars from the About Me menu to set up a photo or image for yourself

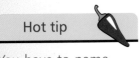

6 You can either upload a picture of yourself and give it a name - the one on the left above is called Sprawk. Or you can choose an image from the options available to you in the drop down menus.

7 This provides you with the potential of three different pictures for different parts of the site

Using the forums

Forums are a very active part of the Saga Zone site. There are forums on all sorts of different topics, and many of these are open to the general public to view – you do not have to be a Saga Zone member to read them.

A good starting point is to have a browse round and see if there are any topics you'd like to contribute to. This is called 'lurking' – reading what others say, but not contributing. The New Members forum in the Community Zone has some useful content, much of which has been supplied by the Saga Zone host.

If you look at any of these Special Interest forums, they follow the same patterns.

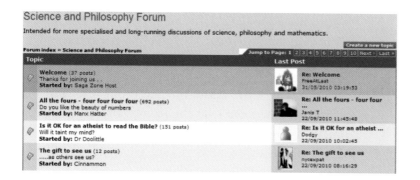

The first posting in the forum is shown on the left, together with the name of the person posting it. The most recent post and the author is shown on the right. Some of the topics have been going a very long time, so, if you want to see comments left some time ago, Jump to Page No.

Don't forget

You can look at what people are saying as much as you like – there is no obligation to contribute.

Don't forget

Check the date of the last posting of a forum you are going to write to. Some will not be read as often as others, but your contribution might reinvigorate the debate!

...cont'd

Posting to forums

1 When you find a forum that you want to contribute to, you can either select the Reply to Topic button at the top of the forum, or you can reply to a particular message

2 From either place, a text box will open for you to write in. Write your comment. You can click Preview to see how it will look

3 It can be useful to include something of the post you are replying to within your own post. (This is particularly helpful if the post was made some time ago, when people might not remember it or have read it.) To do this, Select Quote in the post you are replying to

Re: The gift to see us

[quote name="Cinnammon" time="21/09/2010 @ 15 07 01"]
..walk in another's persons shoes for a day. Would this prevent wars conflicts between religions?
[/quote]

Maybe this will not allow them to understand us, but maybe brilliant for helping us understand them! Perhaps that level of human curiosity and interest would be the best way forward for society, away from the ME society to the How are YOU' society?

4 You can shorten the quote by taking out text you don't want, but make sure the [quote and [/quote] come at the beginning and end of the element you want. Click Preview again to see what it looks like. The quoted text will be in blue

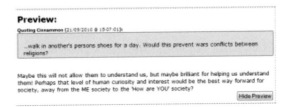

5 When you are happy with what you have written and quoted, press Submit. Your post will be added to the bottom of the thread of comments

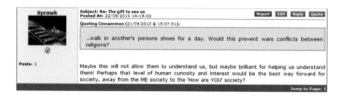

Beware

Posting to a forum will be available to every Saga Zone member, and open forums will be available to any casual visitor to the site.

6 You can go back to Edit your post by clicking on the Edit button. You might want to quote it in replying to someone else's posting, so it is useful to have that button available too

7 Subscribe to a topic by selecting this button at the top of the topic list. You will automatically be contacted when there has been a posting in reply

Subscribe to Topic

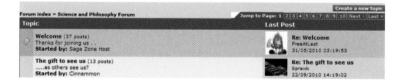

Don't forget

Responding to people who comment on your forum piece keeps the conversation going, and makes the forums more interesting.

For a while, your post will be visible on the topic screen, as shown above, but only until someone replies. It is always the last post for the forum that is shown here. The date and time of the last posting is also shown here, so you can see how active and fast-changing different forums are

115

Starting your own forum

Starting a new topic is easy to do. But just before you do, there are a couple of checks that it makes sense to do. People won't find your topic for a forum if you put it in the wrong place, or if there's already a topic running with a slightly different name.

Hot tip

Choose a name that gives some idea of what the forum is about, so that other users can find it easily.

Beware

It's really important to put a forum in the right section, so check that out carefully before you register your forum.

1 First, look at the Special Interests list on the front page of the forums and decide which section it fits into

Special Interests
- Health
- Money
- Travel
- How To...
- Interests and Hobbies
- Environment
- Gardening
- Technology
- Science and Philosophy Forum
- Leisure
- Relationships
- Life Changes
- Memories
- Working World

2 Select Search from the menu and choose Search the Forums. Type your topic into the text box and see what comes up

Search the Forums

You searched for: Ukulele playing and we found 0 matches.

Type one or more key words in the search for box to search the forums for them. You can also search for a specific display name. By entering both you can find posts containing the keywords posted by the specific person.

Search for

Posted by

Search the Forums

3 Since there are no references to Ukulele, it looks a good target for a new topic

4 Go to the right section - in this case, Index>> Leisure>> Music and press this button

Create a new topic

5 You can now enter information about the topic you want to start

Forum index » Leisure » Music
Create a new topic
Subject *
Description
Message *

6 Type a title for the Subject. Add a short sentence to describe the forum and a message that is no more than 200 words or so to start off the discussion

7 Finishing your post off with a question is a useful way of engaging others

Don't forget

As well as telling others what you think, a forum is about hearing their views too.

8 Check that it looks as you intended, and also that it is in the right section of the forums site. The bread-crumb trail just above the title tells you where it is located.

9 You are automatically Subscribed to the forum as its creator. Check My Responses on the My Zone menu option

When you have created your forum, it will be visible on the Forum Index page because it's new, and to give it a bit more exposure to start it off. These change automatically as new topics are created.

Beware

If someone posts a message you completely disagree with, don't respond to it while you are angry. Think about it, then choose your words carefully.

Joining in the gallery

There is a facility to create an album of your pictures on Saga Zone. You can upload pictures, but this has to be done one at a time. As a result, you are probably only going to want to use this facility in order to share occasional pictures with people on Saga Zone - it's probably not the place for your photo collection overall.

The process is straightforward. You can create your own albums, contribute single images to a public gallery, or take part in the Photo Exhibition. In each case, the process is the same.

Don't forget

You can only upload pictures to the gallery one at a time, so this is best seen as a place to share special pictures with the community.

1 Go to Galleries and select New Album from the menu on the right or Photo Exhibition to enter that

2 Fill in the Title and Description. You can choose to make it visible to everyone, Friends or No One. Select Save

Add a new album
From here you can enter the details of your new album.

Title	Shetland Islands
Description	These are the pictures from a trip I took a couple of summers ago to the Shetland Islands - beautiful - and we were blessed with excellent weather too.
Visibility	Everyone

Save

3 You can now Add a new Picture and set a Category for it too. If you have made the picture visible to everybody then it will be presented in the relevant section as well as in your Album

4 Choose Save and edit to add some text information about the picture

Blogging

A blog is either a sort of public diary, or a place to reflect on things that have been happening in your life, or in the wider world, that you want to share with other people. Click on the Blog button to access the blog section. You can then read latest or popular blogs, and choose Add a new blog to write one of your own.

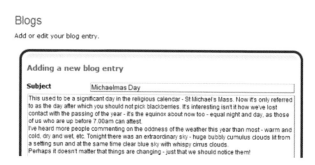

Blogs

Add or edit your blog entry.

Adding a new blog entry

Subject Michaelmas Day

This used to be a significant day in the religious calendar - St Michael's Mass. Now it's only referred to as the day after which you should not pick blackberries. It's interesting isn't it how we've lost contact with the passing of the year - it's the equinox about now too - equal night and day, as those of us who are up before 7.00am can attest.
I've heard more people commenting on the oddness of the weather this year than most - warm and cold, dry and wet, etc. Tonight there was an extraordinary sky - huge bubbly cumulus clouds lit from a setting sun and at the same time clear blue sky with whispy cirrus clouds.
Perhaps it doesn't matter that things are changing - just that we should notice them!

When you have created your blog, there are two settings - one for who is allowed to see the blog and the other for who can comment on the blog. You can also set it so that only you can see it, which could be useful if you wanted to use the tool as a creative diary.

Reading and commenting on blogs

When you read blogs, you can add a comment to them and you can also choose to vote to recommend the blog.

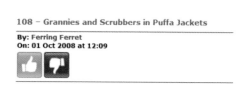

Re: 108 – Grannies and Scrubbers in Puffa Jackets
By christapl On: 02 Oct 2008 09:53
Glad Granny sitting is going OK, it sounds like fun. Great photos it sounds like you had a great time again, its a shame it will be the last one. Do people actually go out in those hats, or is it just for Ascot?
Chris xx

108 – Grannies and Scrubbers in Puffa Jackets

By: Ferring Ferret
On: 01 Oct 2008 at 12:09

You can choose to send your blog to other people within Saga Zone, using the Send Blog To link. People who are not members can read it if you send the browser link.

Hot tip

Look at the number of members that a club has to give you some idea of how active it is.

Don't forget

You are responsible for the behavior of people in your club.

Joining in the clubs

Lots of the clubs on Saga Zone are open to anyone to join. There are some that have restricted membership. The clubs cover all sorts of subjects. Some are clearly very active whilst others have not been visited for some time.

To join an existing club, click on the title. This will take you to the clubhouse where you will find three sections; one to post comments, one for photographs and one for videos.

The menu on the right allows you to explore the different parts of the club. Double click on the pictures in the album to see a larger version and information from the contributor. You can add your own comment below.

Chris295 on 29 Aug 2010

Alf got hold of a bag of poison put out for wild boar by the road where we walk in the mornings. 15 minutes later he was dead. My other two dogs keep looking for him.

Comment **Previous** **Next** **Report Inappropriate**

Comments on Alfie

Alf,

If you see a naughty Jack Russell with big stick up ears its my Pasty so go say hello, he will look after you no problem. AM xx
Aqua Marina on 06 Sep 2010 (19:21)

Start your own club by selecting Open a club from the menu. Name your club and decide whether it is open to all, or just those you have invited. Once the club is open, you will find a very useful Administrator's Guide will give you some tips on the best way to run the club, invite members and how to manage the processes.

Saga Zone social events

The calendar section of the site shows all the events that are happening in the current month.

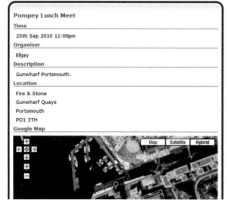

Make sure the event is in the right forum, to ensure that local people see it and can comment on it.

1 Selecting an item on the calendar will open up the information about the event, its time, location, and who is organizing it

2 Select their name to take you to their profile. You can then use this link to contact them about the event. Sometimes they offer an email address instead

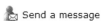 Send a message

Hot tip

It might be best to attend an event that someone else is organizing before you arrange one of your own.

...cont'd

Don't forget

You can see the events that have been organized for the coming months by Selecting the month name on the top right of the calendar.

3 Before you organize your own event, look at the Social Events in the Forums section

Bedfordshire (129 posts)
Started by: FunkyFarmer

Re: Bedfordshire
GenieJean
19/09/2010 20:08:49

any Zoners in or around St Albans/Harpenden/Redbourn/Hemel Hempsted/Watford??? (22 posts)
Started by: Mozzie789

Re: any Zoners in or around
...
TC55
15/09/2010 11:37:03

Essex River Boats (32 posts)
An idea for September
Started by: cjay

Re: Essex River Boats
chrishan
14/09/2010 16:06:24

4 The forum can help to consolidate the plans for the event, which you can then post on the Calendar

5 Fill in the information on the form

6 If you have already set up a forum for the event, check the 'I already have a topic' button

7 If you need to set up a forum, choose the appropriate region for the event

Add an Event

Title

You are limited to 20 Characters

Description

Have you included all the important details?
e.g. Theme / Attire / Reason / Numbers

Venue

Street

Town

Postcode

Time

1st ▼ October ▼ 2010 ▼ 12 ▼ 00 ▼
Start time to expect all participants to have arrived

Forum Thread
☒ I already have a topic
○ I wish to create a topic
○ I do not want a topic

You have the option to attach this event to a thread in the Social Events forum, we recommend that you do this. You can only perform this function if you are the original poster or an admin. Copy the thread link here. ie http://www.sagazone.co.uk/forums /thread/WWWW/ or you can use the thread number at the end of the link (WWWW).

Add My Event

8 LinkedIn, Plaxo and TripIt

These sites have become widely used by the business community, and this chapter explores how you can set up your profile to best effect on each.

Creating a :LinkedIn account

The purpose and benefits of a LinkedIn account depend on good and precise information being provided by all users. It is not quite the same situation as with social networks, such as Facebook and MySpace, which are used for less serious purposes. It is extensively used by people who are self-employed or who work for consultancy companies. There are lots of other people using it too.

The site is one that also offers a paid-for service with additional features. We will focus on the free elements here. The log on process is well supported, with on-screen instructions.

Hot tip

Be clear about whether your account is going to be for business or for you personally.

1   Go to LinkedIn.com and fill in your name, email, and password in the form provided.

2   The next step asks you to choose your working situation, country, zipcode, and industry. Zipcode details are necessary, as information will be provided to you that is geographically linked

Don't forget

If you move, make sure LinkedIn is on the list of places to change your information.

3   The next page offers you an opportunity to identify known colleagues using your email contacts

4 LinkedIn will then ask you to go to your email Inbox and click on the confirmation email to activate the account

5 Once you have done so, you will be asked to complete a security screen to verify your account

Security check
Enter **both words** below, **separated by a space**.
Can't read the words below? Try different words or an audio CAPTCHA.

issuance towering

Text in the box: [   ]

◄ Back   [Sign Up]

By clicking Sign Up, you are indicating that you have read and agree to the Terms of Use and Privacy Policy.

6 LinkedIn offers a screen through which you can add your email contacts. It is able to access webmail addresses (such as GoogleMail or Yahoo, for example). You have to give your email address and password, which it does not store.

Welcome, Anne!

Stay in touch with colleagues and friends
Searching your email contacts is the easiest way to find people you already know on LinkedIn. (eg. hotmail.com, gmail.com, yahoo.com, aol.com)

Your Email: [   ]

Email Password: [   ]

[Continue]

Do you use Outlook, Apple Mail or another email application?
Import your desktop email contacts.

We will not store your password or email anyone without your permission.

Don't forget

Write down your user name and password somewhere safe.

Don't forget

Your email addresses might include lots of people you will not want to have on LinkedIn.

125

...cont'd

Exporting contacts from Outlook

1 To export information from Outlook, open it and select Import and Export from the File menu

2 A wizard will open, and you need to select "Export to a file", and then click "Next"

3 Select "Comma separated values (Windows)" and click "Next"

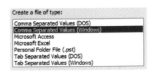

4 Choose the Contacts you would like to export and click "Next"

5 Chose a filename and location to save your file - "Contacts.csv" on the desktop, for example, and click on "Next"

6 Once the data has exported, select the "Choose File" button on the upload page and choose your saved file. Click on the "Upload Contacts" button

7 If it is not possible to upload it when you first try, try again later

Hot tip

Make sure you choose your Contacts folder from Outlook – it won't work if you ask it to search your Inbox.

However you provide email addresses and contact information, LinkedIn will let you know how many of your contacts it already knows, and will encourage you to invite those who are not part of the network to join LinkedIn.

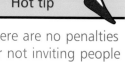
If you identify people who you want to link to or to invite to join LinkedIn, you can then send a personalized email to them. The most efficient way of doing this is to set up your profile first, as this is the hook that all the rest of the activity on site hangs on. The screen below shows how an invitation to link looks, but you will see that the Company information is empty. Once you have filled in your profile, that will not be the case.

Hot tip

Sometimes the connection is not as straightforward as the form suggests. If so, choose 'Other'.

Managing your profile

There are two different ways of going about giving your working life history to LinkedIn - you can upload your CV as a word file and let the clever technology extract the meaningful bits, or you can enter information in different sections yourself. My experience is that my résumé is not in a sufficiently standard format for the service to extract my data correctly, and it looks as though editing it is going to take longer than entering it in the right place to start with. However, there is nothing to be lost by trying the 'upload your résumé' first.

Hot tip

If some of your résumé has been entered in the right format, you can always try saving that and adding other material to it.

1. Identify this element of the screen and click on 'Import your résumé'

2. When it gets it right, the entry might look like this. When it fails to do so, it offers you some text boxes to enter information into

Imported **Educational Advisor Mankoadze Vocational Centre**
Broadcast Media
January 2007 — Present
Edit | Remove this position

Title: Please enter a value.
Company Name: Cottenham Primary Scho
Industry: Broadcast Media
Time Period: ☐ I currently work here
January ▼ 1988 to January ▼ 2001
Description:

3. If it works for you, make sure you click on Save changes at the bottom of the screen

4. If you want to add individual elements of information, work your way through this template

There are some factors that it's helpful to think about when you are completing your profile.

● LinkedIn's 'Import your résumé' feature works best if you have a conventional work pattern, where you work for one company or organization, then move on

● It uses the information you give it about the place you work to add that to the database, so that when the next person fills in the information about the same company, they can match up the two sets of information

● Selecting some of the tick boxes will remove other items from the list. For example, if you select "I currently work here", it removes the second date field from the Time Period section

● As you type in the name of a company or university (called School in the list) it will offer you options to choose from, or you can add a new one

● 'Recommendation' is an interface where you find people that are also on LinkedIn who can endorse the work you have done, so that others can see it. There is a message form that is created that can go to up to 200 people in your network

● The website field allows you to offer links to websites that are relevant - it might be for your company or your own personal website or blog. It provides fields that allow you to comment on your reason for including that particular website

● The link to Twitter allows you to link your twitter contact information with your LinkedIn profile

● The final link is a web address that you can copy and include in emails or other correspondence. You can personalize it, so that it becomes easier to include - http://uk.linkedin.com/in/annesinfo for example

When you have finished, view your full profile as others see it. You can go back and change any fields you don't like.

Don't forget

Make sure you select Save Changes after you've entered each section.

Hot tip

Phoning or talking to people to ask for a recommendation and then emailing them might be a better way of getting a good response.

...cont'd

Further refinements to your data

Once you've got the basic information into LinkedIn, you can start refining it a little.

Make sure you select Save Settings after you've defined who can see your picture.

1 Add a photo to your profile by clicking on the link next to the photo space. Browse for an image in the appropriate format, and select Upload Photo. You can also define who is able to view your photo

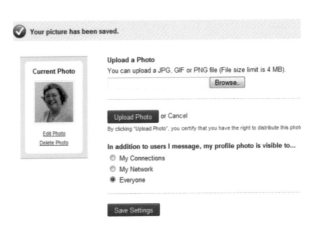

Hot tip

Make sure that the profile information that gives the strongest positive message about you comes at the top of the profile page.

2 Changing the order of your profile information is a straightforward process. You might want to move areas without content down to the bottom of the page. There is a cross to the left of each title. Select the cross or on the section title. The section text will become grey and a box will appear around it. Keeping the left mouse button down, drag the text up or down the list to the position where you want it to be, and release the left mouse button

3 Contacts through LinkedIn are all email based. It is possible to fill in the information about your contact details - phone number and address. This is not generally a problem if that information is about a company, but you might want to be cautious about putting personal contact details online here

Settings: what they mean

You can access the settings page from the Settings option on the top right of the menu. The page is divided into sections, each describes the access and openness of the information you have provided. It is perhaps helpful to consider how LinkedIn sees its network, as this will perhaps help you to decide how open you want to be.

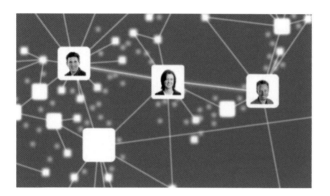

Don't forget

This is only a model – actually, links between people can be very complex, but it's useful to think about how you are linked to people in your business organization, and how their links relate to yours.

This diagram comes from a LinkedIn video and illustrates their perception of the network. If you see yourself as one of the people shown above, you will have links radiating out to other people, who themselves have links to other people. The intention of LinkedIn is that it should make it easier to find people with common or compatible business interests. This will only happen if each shares enough information with others.

Profile Settings

The default setting for the profile area is to make it visible to everyone. Different headings here allow you access to change the data you've input about yourself.

The Manage Recommendations heading allows you to manage recommendations you may already have received from others, and encourages you to ask your connections for recommendations and endorsements. This is an area that the readers of your profile will find useful, especially if the endorsements come from people they respect or who occupy significant roles within organizations.

Hot tip

If some of your résumé has been entered in the right format, you can always try saving that, and then adding other material to it.

...cont'd

The Member Feed visibility field describes who can see your updates. You can think of them as a widening circle, as shown in this diagram.

Email Notifications

This section of the settings controls how many emails you are likely to receive and from whom, as this chart shows. You can choose to read all the messages on the website, if you choose. Some of the services are only available if you upgrade to the paid-for site subscription.

Hot tip

Getting emails when contacts do things can be helpful as a way of keeping in touch without having to go to the site all the time.

		Individual Email Send emails to me immediately	Daily Digest Email Send one bundle per day	Weekly Digest Email Send one bundle email per week	No Email Read messages on the website
General					
InMails, Introductions, and OpenLink	?	●	Not Available	○	○
Invitations	?	●	Not Available	○	○
Profile Forwards	?	●	Not Available	○	○
Job Notifications	?	●	Not Available	○	○
Questions from your Connections	?	●	Not Available	○	○
Replies/Messages from connections	?	●	Not Available	○	○
Network Updates	?	Not Available	Not Available	●	○
Referral Center Messages	?	Not Available	Not Available	●	○
Discussions					
Network Update Activity	?	●	Not Available	Not Available	○
Groups					
Invitations to join groups	?	●	Not Available	○	○
Group Digest Emails	?				

Home Page Settings

This control sets what information is seen on your home page, in particular, it shows people who have a connection to you.

RSS Settings

If you are someone who uses RSS feeds, you can control how LinkedIn accesses those here, and what feeds are displayed on your home page.

Groups

This control sets whether you are receiving group invitations, and allows you to control how they are presented to you.

Personal Information

This section allows you to change your name and location, email address and password, and to close your account if you so wish.

Privacy Settings

This section controls what you can see from other people, and what the system tells other people about you. So, for example, you can decide whether research surveys can find you and invite you to take part. You can decide to allow visitors to your page to browse through your connections. Click on the blue headings to open the page to access the controls.

My Network

This determines what it is that people are told you are looking for – Find a job, Hire employees, Investigate deals with companies, and so on. Some of them are mutually exclusive, so it's important to get these set so that a realistic purpose for your use of LinkedIn appears on your Profile information.

The biggest advantage of LinkedIn as a service is that, as long as people keep their information up-to-date, you will be able to find them even if they move jobs. The next section looks at some special features and ways of using them.

Don't forget

You can make setting choices now, use them for a while, and then adjust them later.

Hot tip

If your work colleagues are also on LinkedIn, make sure that what LinkedIn says you're looking for will not cause you any problems. You might not want your current employer to think you are looking for another job.

Finding people

1 Start by inviting people to connect on LinkedIn. Make sure you send a personal message, to encourage them to respond

2 As your network develops, you can find people by company, location or industry and see their information at a glance. You can then contact them, either directly through LinkedIn or through their email connection. You can also use this information to pass on to others, or to use it for any marketing activity you might be engaged in.

3 Another way of identifying more people to join your network is to explore the Add Connections part of the Contacts menu. The people listed have shared connections. The "2nd" icon next to their name indicates their closeness to you. If they were a direct contact, they'd have a "Ist"

Hot tip

The numbers should not be a discouragement from contacting someone. Just because they are a contact of a contact does not mean you might not be able to do business together.

4 The information about how many shared contacts there are is also useful. If you click on the number of shared contacts, you can see who they are

Hot tip

If you know one of your shared contacts well, you might want to talk to them before contacting the new person.

5 You can click on any of their photos to open their profile and, therefore, be able to send them an invitation to link, or a direct message

135

Groups

Groups are a positive element of the facilities offered by LinkedIn. There are many thousands of them, exploring a vast variety of subjects and with a very diverse range of members. There are groups that operate in a significant number of other languages – 763 in Portuguese, for example as well as over 38,000 in English.

Some of the groups have an official endorsement from an organization – the White House, for example. But there are sites for Canon or Mac users, Milwaukee Brewers Fans, and so on.

From the initial search process, you can find similar groups that extends your search into the range of groups that could be related to the first group you found. So, for example, from Milwaukee Brewers Fans, this is a list of some of the groups that are offered.

There are groups that are more 'hobby' based, but these generally offer a professional view of that hobby. So 'knitting', for example, identifies the Textile and Carpet Manufacturer's Network, Design Sourcing, Natural material supplier for small business, and so on.

As well as the general search for groups, there is a section of the menu called 'Groups You May Like' which takes an intelligent view of your profile information and the people you are networked with, then offers you a selection of groups that you may want to join. The information about the group shows who owns it and the membership numbers.

Hot tip

'Groups You May Like' has some really interesting groups you might never have thought of searching for.

...cont'd

Group membership

Groups can either be open to any LinkedIn member to join, or can require new members to request to join. There is then a process by which the group manager can approve the new member. Once you have joined a group, you will get email communication in your email inbox when new posts are made to the group.

Discussions (1)

Ref - The Classroom Experiment. Why the prime time media focus on fairly well know classroom 'tips and tricks', when there are excellent examples of transfm learning being embedded globally.

Comment or flag »

Started by Roland Meredith, Leadership and Education Consultant at Leadership and Learning Futures

Selecting the link to the right of this message will take you into LinkedIn and, at the point you could immediately post a comment.

If there is a group you have joined and you think other people you know would like to join it, you can send them a message by clicking on Share on the group listing. Select the icon to the right of the "To" box to see your connections and choose who you would like to invite. You can personalize the message too.

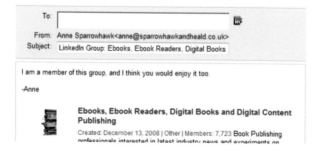

To:

From: Anne Sparrowhawk<anne@sparrowhawkandheald.co.uk>

Subject: LinkedIn Group: Ebooks, Ebook Readers, Digital Books

I am a member of this group, and I think you would enjoy it too.

-Anne

Ebooks, Ebook Readers, Digital Books and Digital Content Publishing
Created: December 13, 2008 | Other | Members: 7,723 Book Publishing professionals interested in latest industry news and experiments on

Within a group, you can see who the members are, and choose to 'follow' them. This means that you are notified of activities they complete on LinkedIn, and, similarly, they get to see what you have been doing if they are following you. You can turn following off by selecting Stop following.

...cont'd

Starting your own group

This is a straightforward process, filling in the template offered from the Create a Group tab on the Groups menu.

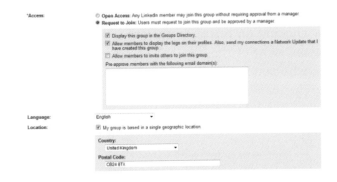

The form allows you to classify your group and add a logo, summary of the groups purpose, and a description.

You can also set the language, geographical location, and access arrangements.

You can then invite people from your connections list to join your group, and also people who are not LinkedIn members via email addresses. The management tools offer a range of ways of managing people joining the group, the content they post, and the creation of group rules and policies. You can change owner too.

Jobs and More

Selecting Jobs from the main menu presents you with a list of jobs currently available, or a search box to search by company name or job title.

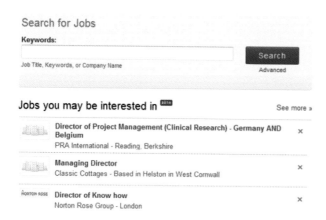

Some industries use LinkedIn very actively, as a way of finding potential new employees informally.

Choosing 'See more' provides a further list. Choose 'Find people in your network' to identify people who you may know or know second hand that work at that company, and who you could contact for some more inside information.

Research Director
River Research - London, United Kingdom - Sep 2, 2010
Find people in your network at River Research

Julian Kenway
Partner &
Co-Founder at River
Research
2nd

LinkedIn as a free service allows you to ask for up to 5 introductions. If you find someone you want to contact who is known by one of your contacts, you can use this message template. It asks your contact to send your message on to the person you want to get to know.

Hot tip

Use your Introductions carefully as this is a limited service, unless you decide to pay for LinkedIn on a monthly basis.

...cont'd

The More menu options

There are a number of powerful resources available from this menu option, described here in outline.

- 'Companies' offers a route into companies that you might be interested in, and allows you to find people in your network who have a connection with that company

- 'Answers' is a place where you can post questions on almost any topic and get an intelligent answer. Topics include technology questions, legalities of royalty payments, and many other listed topics

- 'Direct Ads' allows you to place an advert on LinkedIn and gives you choices about where it will appear and who will be told about it

- 'Learning Center' offers information about how to use LinkedIn, and provides detailed user guides

- 'Reading List' by Amazon is an affiliated service for LinkedIn. It encourages people to give book recommendations, and you can see what people you have been following have been reading, or what the major book trends are at any one time

- 'Events' offers a list of events that might be relevant to you. You can see who from your network might be attending, allowing you to share plans for visiting

- 'My Travel' is a link to a tool called TripIt, on which you can record future trips, and you can see who in your network might be in the same area at the same time

- 'Upgrade my account' allows you to upgrade to a paid-for service. This adds a number of features, and facilitates direct email communication through InMail, and significantly more information about how your profile and details are being reviewed

- 'The Application Directory' offers a range of free to use tools, of which Amazon is one; they include a calendar, file system, blog link, and a number of others

Creating a Plaxo account

The focus of Plaxo as a site is to be a single site where you have all your contact details in one place, and up-to-date. Since this service is online, you will then be able to access it wherever you are, and be confident that it will have the appropriate contact details for the person you want to communicate with.

1 To start your Plaxo account, go to www.plaxo.com

2 There are two options there. Either fill in the form provided, or you can link straight into Plaxo through your existing Facebook account

Beware

If you have more than one Facebook account, make sure you use the right one to verify your TripIt account.

3 When you have filled that form in and sent it off, Plaxo will send an email for you to confirm and activate your account

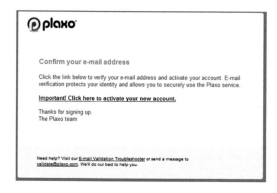

Finding people in Plaxo

1 When you activate your account, you are asked about importing names from your address book, first on webmails

2 If you have an Outlook account then choose the bottom option the opportunity to import addresses from Outlook will be offered. You have to download a program to do that

3 Download the program. It will probably be saved by your browser. Then run the program. A progress bar will show how effectively the program is accessing your Outlook address book and harvesting information from that

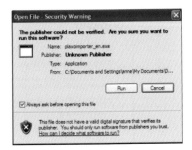

Whichever sort of address book it has been searching through, it will then provide you with a list of contacts, some that it already knows all about, and some that it would like you to invite to join Plaxo.

Hot tip

These distinctions are not always clear in life, so think about the groups of people you would be likely to invite to different types of events and categorize them accordingly.

As with other services, you can select the names of the people already known to Plaxo and invite them to connect to you. As you set up the connection, you can set them as one of three types of relationship – Business, Friends and Family.

If you invite someone from your address book who would be new to Plaxo, you do not have to categorize them until they agree to link with you.

Completing your profile

Plaxo offers the opportunity to complete profile information about your education, work history and current working activity. You can make this available to different audiences. The personal contact details allow you the greatest specificity of profiling, as shown here. The other elements of your profile do not include Any Plaxo member as a group distinct from Everyone.

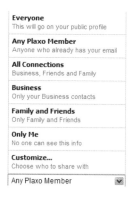

Don't forget

Don't forget to select Save changes when you've added more information to any section of the profile.

Other features Plaxo offers

Plaxo provides a powerful tool to allow you to identify connections and to inform you when people you might want to connect to have added their details to the database. So you might be offered information about links to past school or college contacts, work colleagues, and so on.

The More option from the tool bar offers some other useful tools.

- There is a calendar feature, which you can share with others in Plaxo

- The tool to access your connections list is on this menu

- There is a tool to choose, create and send ecards to people online - both Plaxo and non-Plaxo people

- The group option is available from this menu. It allows you to create groups for many different purposes. You can control what the visibility of the group is - whether it is Public, Moderated or Private

- You can access your profile from this menu, and it also provides a link to a gallery where you can upload photographs, if you choose to. These can then be viewed by groups or individuals that you designate.

Plaxo paid-for services

If you upgrade to a paid-for service from Plaxo, your email contacts, whether they be from Outlook or a Google service, can be automatically kept in sync. Also a back-up and de-duplication of addresses service is provided, and you can arrange to have unlimited e-cards and a version of Plaxo to run on your smartphone.

TripIt

This is a tool that has been integrated within LinkedIn, but is also available as a standalone product. It provides a service where you can share your travel plans with others. It also helps you to manage your travel arrangements, and can be useful if the plans have to change.

1 Sign up for TripIt by going to www.tripit.com and either entering your email and creating a password, or using your Facebook or Google login

Beware

If you have more than one Facebook account, make sure you use the right one to verify your TripIt account.

Sign up for TripIt

> Email
>
> Password
>
> ☑ Send me TripIt updates and tips
>
> **Sign up - it's free!**
>
> Or, sign up with...
>
> Google   Google Apps
>
> Facebook
>
> By clicking Sign Up, you confirm that you accept the User Agreement. We don't share your email address. More info

2 If you have signed in with your email and password, then TripIt will need to verify your account, and will send you a message asking you to confirm your account through your email. If you sign up through the other services, it will verify your account using their records as confirmation

TripIt

Thanks for signing up!
We need to verify your email address. Check your email for a message from us and click on the verification link.

Don't see it? Check your spam folder or contact us for assistance.

Hot tip

Have a look at the Apps menu on the top right of the screen for some useful tools to make managing your trip easier.

Hot tip

TripIt works best as a networking program, when you enter trips well in advance and can coordinate plans with others.

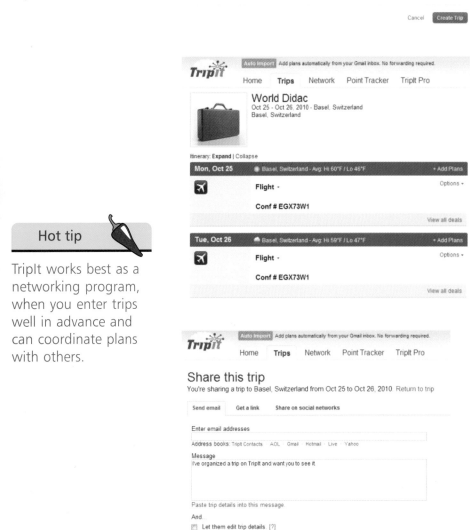

Create a trip. You can either do this manually or, alternatively, TripIt can import data that you have in Gmail and extract the relevant data from that.

If you enter a confirmation number from a flight booking from any airline that it knows about (and that seems to be most of them), it will manage that data for you.

Once you've created your trip, you can share its details with specific friends and family, or more widely on your network.

9 Sharing your Ideas

Your ideas might be written, digital photos or movies, and these can all be shared with a worldwide audience or a more select group of friends and family, as this chapter describes.

Blogging sites

The first thing you need to do to make your blog a success is to decide the purpose of the site, and the features you will want to use.

Why you want to blog

- To share your thoughts with a limited and private audience, or, alternatively, a wider group of readers

- To support the activities of a club or sports group

- To allow a community an opportunity of publicizing the events that are happening there

- To share knowledge of a specialist area with people everywhere

- To have a focus and purpose for writing

Choosing a blogging tool

Whatever the reason, choosing your blogging tool is an important starting point. The table opposite compares the two main free blogging tools, and will help you make the decision. Some features they both share, in addition to the obvious ones of writing frames and the opportunity to add pictures, are multiple authors, spam filters for comments from readers and email posting.

If you are new to computing, Blogger offers the easiest interface and starting point. It allows you to create your own domain name (web address) and, provided it is something very specific, it is likely that the name would be available. So, for example, if you wanted to be http://CommunityName.blogspot.com then Blogger.com makes that very easy. It allows you to add adverts to the page, with a potential for earning money if users click on them.

Wordpress.com is also a free tool, though you can upgrade to a paid-for service that offers more features and resources. It also has a sister product, wordpress.org, that provides you with blogging software that you can host on your own server if you want.

Don't forget

You can also use other social networks like Facebook and Saga Zone to blog.

Feature	Blogger.com	Wordpress.com
Templates and design formats	Blogger has easy-to-customize templates	Templates are fixed but up to 100 themes are offered with some additional customization
Domain names	You can set the domain name when you set up your blog	You have to upgrade to a paid-for account to set the domain name
Image storage	1 Gigabyte	3 Gigabytes
Static pages	10 static pages can be created to give information about your blog	Static pages can be created and listed in separate menus
Upload from email	Can submit blog posts by email	Blog posts and images can be uploaded from email
Team blogs	Two types of user group — administrators and non-administrators — are supported	Four types of user group — administrator, editor, author and contributor
Reader's input	All comments come into a single box for review, but you cannot edit the comments posted	Blog administrator can edit comments and set up moderation too
Spam filtering	Applied to comments automatically	Spam protection provided
Privacy settings	You can restrict access to invited only Googlemail account holders	Individual posts can be password protected or Private

Hot tip

If you are thinking about using another blogging service, then use the headings here to see how it matches up.

149

...cont'd

There are a number of other sites that you might explore too.

Don't forget

Your readership will depend on where you post your blog, as well as what you write about.

- www.blogsome.com, where you can choose your own web address and some themes for the pages

- livejournal.com is a site that is more community focused and requires payment for some of the features it offers

- spaces.msn.com is the blog that is associated with MySpace. It generally has a younger audience as a result

- 360.yahoo.com is the site offered by Yahoo and relates well to Flickr, if photographs are a major interest for you, then this site might be the best option for a blog

Whatever you choose you'll need to be organized
Whichever site you choose to use, there are some common processes and steps that need to be followed. The following pages are going to focus on the details of setting up a blog on www.Blogger.com, but similar processes apply to almost any of the tools.

- Register with a site/tool

- Choose a name for your blog and a domain name for it

- Decide on the style and template you want to use

- Set up a page with a number of features

- Think about ways to publicize your blog and communicate with others. Make them happen

- Understand the feedback you get from reader's comments

Hot tip

Read other people's blogs to help you. What features do they use that you really like?

If you are going to be a serious blogger, then it is certainly worth spending a while exploring Blogger.com first and then reviewing other sites to see if you need the additional features they offer. One of the real benefits of this approach is that it is very easy to get started with Blogger, and once you've started to explore what you want to say and do, it will be clear what additional features you want to implement to get the most out of your blog.

Setting up your blog

1 Go to www.blogger.com. It is a service provided by Google. If you already have a google email, then you can log in with your Google log in details. If not, click on this button to progress to the account page

> **CREATE A BLOG**

2 Set up the information for your Google account, or just enter the information needed for a Blog account

1 NAME BLOG ▷ **2** CHOOSE TEMPLATE

1 **Name** your blog

Blog title

Your blog's title will appear on your published blog, on your dashboard and in your profile.

Blog address (URL)   http:// [   ] .blogspot.com
Check Availability

The URL you select will be used by visitors to access your blog. **Learn more**

Word Verification

Type the characters you see in the picture.

CONTINUE

Hot tip

Make sure you've written down the name of the blog and the web address so that you can find it again.

3 The name of the blog and the address it uses are two separate things. The name is not compared or checked with others on the web, whilst the website address has to be. You may need to opt for something else if the name you choose is not available. Enter the security text and press Continue.

...cont'd

4 The next step is to choose the template you would like to use for the site. Press Continue

5 You can now choose to either customize your site further, or begin blogging. Choose Start Blogging

Writing your first blog

While blogs are freer in form that most social network sites, they do offer text boxes as means of your entering text. The tool bar on the top of the text box does allow you to input images, video and also website links as well. If you are HTML competent, you can edit the page using that format as well.

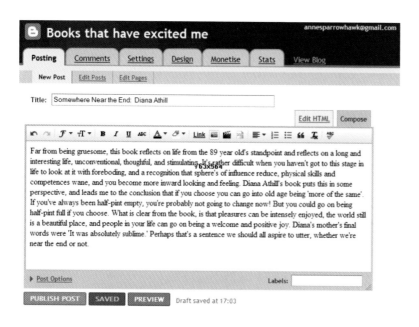

> **Hot tip**
>
> Use the spell check provided; some blog readers are very upset by poor spelling!

153

When you have written your text, you have the option to publish the posting, to save it or to preview. Preview allows you to have a look at how it appears on screen before publishing it to the Internet. You can then change the font size, or add a picture, or whatever changes you want to make.

> **Hot tip**
>
> Use the site name, or some other text, rather than the full URL as the blog link. That makes it much easier to read.

1 Select these buttons to add a link to a webpage, a photograph or a video

2 Select the Link button, which opens a screen where you can put the text link you want as well as the weblink.

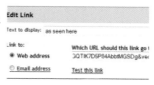

...cont'd

Beware

Some web links don't last very long - people change the page very frequently. Make sure you are linking to a page that will last.

3 Select Test this link to make sure that the link works

4 Upload an image or video from your hard drive by choosing the appropriate button

5 If you add a picture into the text box, you can center, right or left justify the image, but you will not be able to add text to the right or left of it unless you edit the HTML

Designing your blog page

1 Select the Design tab from the blog editor. Use this page to add gadgets and change the layout of your blog

Hot tip

Add gadgets from time to time – your readers will enjoy that. Too many all at once can be very confusing.

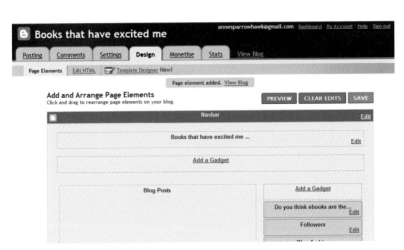

2 Select Add a Gadget to find a menu of tools that you might find useful - polls, lists, picture links, and many others in the More Gadgets section

3 Select the rectangle with an active gadget and, keeping the mouse button down, move to your preferred location

4 When you have made the additions and changes you want, select the orange Save button at the top right. You can then view the changes that have been made and go round the loop again until you have your page content as you want it

5 Select the Template Designer link underneath the Design tab to change the color and style of your blogs

6 The menu to the left of the scroll bar tells you which element of the Blog you will be changing. When you have made changes to the fonts used or color applied, then choose the Apply to Blog button to see how your changes look.

7 If you choose, you can also add adverts to your blog page. Blogger is linked to Adsense. You have to set up an Adsense user account following the instructions on screen. Layout options are offered and implemented on your blog page, as you can see below

MONDAY, 13 SEPTEMBER 2010

World Without End - Ken Follett

"Does it need to be this thick?" The question a friend asked me about this book. It's the second about medieval Kingsbridge by this author, and I sort of think it does need to have this length in order to create a

Create a blog
It's easy and it only takes a minute
www.blogger.com

Settings you can control

Beware

Don't include people in your automatic email list who would be annoyed by receiving regular mails from you. Ask them first!

The Settings tab offers you a number of menu options to control, which provides tools to manage the site. Click Save Settings at the bottom of each page to save your changes.

● Basic allows you to title the site and allow search engines to find your site

● Publishing allows you to change where the site is posted

● Formatting sets the date formats, time zone, language, as well as setting the structure of the layout

● Comments controls who can comment, and the way in which they are displayed. It also allows you to set up ten email addresses of people who will be automatically emailed when a comment has been posted. This can be useful for team or community blogs

● Archiving allows you to decide how often the blog will be archived

● The site feed tab allows Google Blog search to monitor your blog and then publish the results

● The Email and Mobile tab allows you to set up an automatic email to go to ten favorite readers every time you update your blog, and also controls how you update your blog from your email. If you want to access your blog from a phone, then you add that here

● OpenID lets one site you have subscribed to communicate about your account with another

● Permissions allows you to sanction up to 100 people to contribute to your blog, and also defines who can read it. It is set to anybody by default

Your profile

1 Select Design from the top menu bar of Blogger

2 The menu bar changes. Now select Dashboard

3 This brings up a summary of your current account information. Select Edit Profile

4 This opens up a screen in which you can edit different elements of your user profile. When you have worked your way down it, select this button to save your changes

5 View Profile will take you to the screen that now reflects your profile

6 Revisit your blog page and you will now see that your profile has changed, and clicking on View my complete profile will take the user to a page which compiles all the information about you

Beware

Don't give away personal and contact details in your profile information.

Don't forget

People like to know something about the author of the blog they are reading.

Your readers

From the edit menu, you can access two other tabs that show you where your readers come from. This screen from part of the Stats menu shows which countries they are from and which browsers are being used to view your pages.

The Comments tab allows you to manage comments people leave on your blog, so you can remove unwanted or inappropriate messages. Ultimately, you might hope to

have people who are 'following' you. You can try this out by choosing Follow on the top menu bar.

Encouraging people to follow you by linking to other social networks that you belong to will increase the number of people who find your blog and follow it. This is discussed further in Chapter 12.

Creating a Flickr account

Flickr is the most widely used photo account and is linked to Yahoo. Google has Picasa as its service, which integrates with its other services too. Flickr seems to be the most popular program to support community use, and has the easiest interface to manage.

1 Go to www.flickr.com and select this button

Create Your Account

2 You will be asked to sign in to a Yahoo account. If you do not have one, select this button and fill in the application

Don't have a Yahoo! ID?
Signing up is easy.
Sign Up

3 Once you have signed in, you will arrive at the home page where you will be greeted – the language changes often!

 Jambo anne.sparrowhawk
Now you know how to greet people in Swahili

4 Choose this button to open the Upload interface

Upload

5 Choose this button and navigate to the location on your computer where you have some images you want to use – 10 to 15 for now

Step 1:
Choose photos and videos [link]
Note: Videos are limited to 90 seconds in length, and 150MB in filesize. Learn more »

6 Select the images (using Ctrl Shift if you want to highlight a number at once) and click Open

7 The files will be listed and the privacy set to public. Choose this button to upload your first set of images

Beware

Flickr does have a limit of showing you only the last 200 images you upload. If you are going to be a serious user, it is worth upgrading by paying the relatively small annual charge and removing all size restrictions.

159

Don't forget

The upload will take longer if you upload lots of pictures at once.

Managing your pictures

Now you have uploaded some sample images to try out the site with, we will go through a number of different processes with these images so that you will be able to decide how best to organize your pictures when you upload more. The photographs are seen as a batch so you can do things with them as a whole group. A tag can apply to the batch or to an individual photograph.

 Click on this message to go to **add a description**, the Batch operations page

 The photographs are seen as group because they have been uploaded together. Any tag you apply will be added to all the pictures

Add Tags [2]

coast-to-coast walk, Yorkshire, landscape   ADD

Titles, descriptions, tags

Title: Valley in the mist

Description: Looking to the East as we set off

Tags: "Coast-to-coast walk" Yorkshire landscape

Title: Upper Swaledale

Description: Swaledale opens out and the flat valley bottom is apparent

Tags: "Coast-to-coast walk" Yorkshire landscape

Title: Walkers united

Description: All present and correct

Tags: "Coast-to-coast walk" Yorkshire landscape

 The tags were applied to the whole set. You can add a title to each picture, together with any descriptive text you want. Press Save at the bottom

SAVE

4 You now have a Photostream that you can organize. Click on this button in the top menu to open the Organize function

Organize & Create

Don't forget

Even though you might be managing your photo collection on Flickr, it's essential to have a copy of all the photographs on your computer too.

5 Drag single pictures, or a whole group of pictures, onto the Batch Organize space. This menu allows you to choose groups easily

6 Use the Permissions menu to set the access for the pictures on the photos in the batch

7 You can edit the date, to set the exact date for all the pictures as a batch

8 Use the Add People and Add Tags options to label all the photographs with the name of a person or tag – event name, and so on

Hot tip

Labeling people in photographs means you can find all of the shots of a particular person, no matter when they were taken.

9 Use the Add to set menu to create a new set of pictures you can name

161

Sets of pictures

1 Open the Sets menu from the top menu bar

2 This is the interface where you can select the pictures you want to use to make up the set, and to add some text about it

3 Here you can name the set and choose one of the pictures to represent it

4 Open a set by double clicking on the picture used to represent it

5 Use the Arrange menu to organize the order in which the pictures within the set will be presented

6 The Batch edit tools offer facilities that can be applied to all the photos in the set. Select Add items to the map to locate your pictures on the world map

7 Home down on the location of a photo you want to map by using the left right arrows and magnification tool. You can move the map using the left mouse button. When you have found your photo's location, drag and drop it into place

Sharing your pictures

Many people only use Flickr so they can share their pictures with friends and family. Creating a group to do that online is a very effective way of sharing pictures without having to email attachments to different people, and can achieve the same security too.

Making a friends and family group

1 Choose the Groups item from the menu

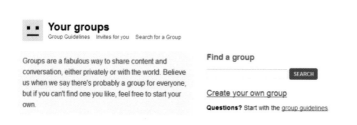

Don't forget

You can add further people to your group whenever you want, and you don't have to include everyone to start with.

2 From this screen, choose the Create your own group item and, on the next screen, select Private. This is the ideal one for friends and family. You will see that it cannot be changed to a more public group later.

3 You might want to have a group for a specific event or just a joint family album. You can describe it's purpose here.

4 You are expected to apply filters to material you upload to Flickr, so that adult material is marked as such. Pictures have to be graded, even in a private site.

...cont'd

5 Click Next. If a group with the title you have chosen already exists, you will be invited to create a new group name.

6 Specify the titles for Admin and members of your group and then select All Done

Administrators of Sparrowhawk Family Album will be called:

Sprawks Admin

Moderators of Sparrowhawk Family Album will be called:

Members of Sparrowhawk Family Album will be called:

Sprawks Member

ALL DONE

Don't forget

You might want to include a photograph that is typical of the sort of Group you are going to be, rather than for a particular event or place.

7 The group administration page will then open, where you can add a group icon and create a web address that you can give to anyone to view your items

8 You can add your group icon from your computer. Choose a photograph or other image from your computer or other location and edit it by moving the highlighting square in the lower image around to represent your group

 To the left is what your buddy icon will look like. You can drag around and resize the square below to get it just how you like it. When you are happy with your icon, click the pink button to the right.

☒ constrain selection to square

 MAKE THE ICON

CANCEL

Managing your members

As the group administrator, you can invite Flickr members to join the group and also invite people who are not yet Flickr users.

1 Select Contacts from the top menu bar

A Flickr member?

You can invite any Flickr member to join a group, whether or not they are your contacts.

You'll be able to select people and send them a customized invitation to join Sparrowhawk Family Album.

Invite a Flickr member?

or...

A friend who isn't a member yet?

Inviting a friend to join a group is a good way to get them to join Flickr and get involved in a group they might be interested in.

When you invite a new person to join up via a group, we set you up as contacts, and add them as a new member of Sparrowhawk Family Album.

Invite a new person to join Flickr?

2 You can invite a Flickr user by giving their Flickr name, email address or full name. Your Flickr profile does not necessarily have your name in it, so the screen invites you to give your full name and type a message to explain your group's aims

3 To invite people who are not Flickr subscribers, you need to create an invitation, and there is a form which you can personalize to do that

165

Don't forget

People can be invited to join your group at any time. They have to create a Flickr account to become full members.

First, enter your friends' info

1 Email Address
anne@themollers.net
Name (required)
Anne Moller
☐ This person is a friend.
☐ This person is family.

2 Email Address
Mary6271@yahoo.co.uk
Name (required)
Mary Mcnee
☐ This person is a friend.
☐ This person is family.

3 Email Address

Name (required)

☐ This person is a friend.
☐ This person is family.

Or, go advanced...

You can also find your friends on Flickr using your address book from Yahoo! Mail or other online services.

Then, customize your invitation and send it

This invitation will be coming from you. But we don't know your full name and that is a bit weird for the recipient. You can go and add it to your profile first or you can just enter it in this box and we will use it for this invitation but won't save it on your profile.

Your Name: anne.sparrowhawk

To: Anne Moller <anne@themollers.net>, Mary Mcnee <Mary6271@yahoo.co.uk>

From: anne@sparrowhawkandheald.co.uk

Subject: [Flickr] anne.sparrowhawk has invited you to join Sparrowhawk Family Album

Hi,

I wanted to invite you to join a cool group on Flickr! It's called Sparrowhawk Family Album, and it's a big bunch of fun!

If you would like to join this group, click on the following link (or copy and paste it into your web browser). Then you can see what this group is all about!

http://flickr.com/welcome/example/

See you on Flickr!

anne.sparrowhawk

Joining other groups

There are many other groups that you can join. If you search for Landscape photographs, for example, you will be offered a range of groups of varying sizes and with certain specific interests.

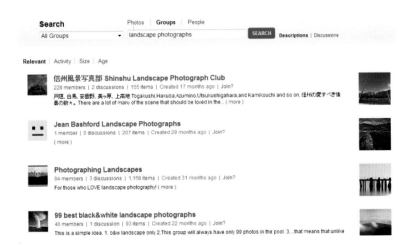

Clicking on More, or on the group name, will pull up a screen with the Group Pool where you can link to individual contributors through their images. You can also ask to join the group and find out more about them.

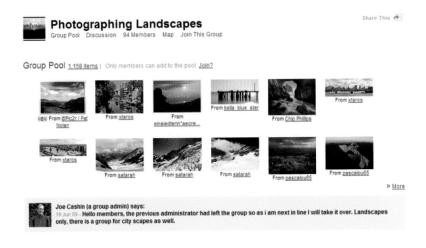

Photographs are not restricted to one group, so you can share your best images with a number of groups, if you want to.

Joining YouTube

Whilst some people do use Flickr for managing and sharing their videos, the site that most people use to share moving images of all sorts is YouTube. It has a vast collection of music, TV programs, educational animations and videos, as well as home-grown movies of all sorts. Unlike most of these sites, you are welcome to review videos without becoming a YouTube member.

To join the site, you do the following.

1 Go to www.youtube.com

2 Select Create Account

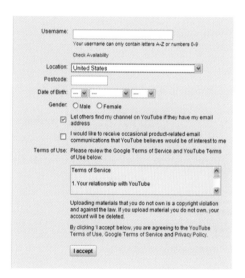

3 Complete the information in the dialog box above. If you choose a user name that is not available, it will offer you an alternative. The terms of service is detailed and you are advised to print it out. You accept the terms of service in order to confirm the account

4 When you enter the site, you will be able to view video materials as before. Choose Upload

167

Hot tip

Remember to keep your user name and password somewhere safe, especially if it offers you a name to use.

Uploading a video

You can upload video either as a file from your computer, or directly from a webcam. The webcam can record and upload as it is doing so.

In order to upload a video file you have on your computer, you need to do the following.

1 Select Upload from the top menu bar

2 Select this button on the next screen   Upload video

3 From your computer's file menu, find the file you want to upload and open it

4 The file then uploads and a message indicates its progress. The site then processes the video and you can fill in details about it in the dialog box below

5 When the upload has completed, the address and preview of the video will appear at the top of the screen. Click on the address given to see your uploaded video

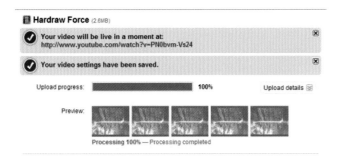

 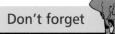
6 This address can also be embedded into a website or blog that you control. The address and embedding html string appears below

7 Set the privacy settings to suit your needs, and click Save Changes to save the video and its data

8 Scroll down and repeat the process if you want to upload further videos

9 Click on the link to view the video. It will appear alongside other videos of a similar subject

You can then make some changes to control how other people view your video and what they are allowed to do with it. It is important that you do not put up videos that you do not have the copyright for. Movies that you have taken yourself are, of course, fine. As with photographs on Flickr, you can also edit the information about the video, and add information about where it was taken.

Adding information

There are a number of controls that are available to change the way your video appears, and to give it additional features.

- The 'Info and Settings' tab allows you to edit the text you have entered about your video. It also offers a range of options for determining who can search for and view the video, and who can make comments about it. It also allows you to decide whether everyone can take this video and embed it on their page

- 'AudioSwap' allows you to add a musical track to your video. Select the audio track you want from the list offered, and then Preview with the selected track. Once you have clicked Publish, you cannot go back to your original sound recording

- 'Annotations' provides you with a tool to view your video and then, at places you choose, to put speech bubbles or notes to explain or describe your video further. A timeline tool is provided under the video, which you can zoom into to make your comments more precise. You should Publish it when you are happy with your changes

- 'Captions and subtitles' is an opportunity for you to add a file of subtitles or transcript to the video. Select Add a Caption Track for specific information about how to do this

- When you select 'View' on video page, you go to the page where your video is normally seen. Here you can edit all the above tabs again

Select Save Changes. You can also use the Map Location button to save the geographical location of the video. Use Search to enter the name of the relevant town.

Don't forget

It is possible to add captions or annotations at any time after the video has been uploaded.

My Channel and Subscribers

1 Click on the right arrow next to your account name on the top right of the screen

2 Select Account. Here you can change the photograph used for your profile, and add personal information about yourself

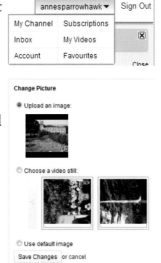

3 The account setting options on the left allow you to change privacy and email settings, as well as information about you that visitors will see

4 When you have changed any of these settings, remember to select Save Changes

5 Select My Channel from the menu. You can create a bulletin in which you can send messages, and links to your latest videos. You can change the color too

Beware

Remember not to put personal contact details here for all to see.

...cont'd

6 The Modules tab allows you to decide on the modules that will make up your bulletin

7 The Videos and Playlists tab controls the video materials that will be referred to within your bulletin

8 When you have created the bulletin, write a message and select Post Bulletin. Anyone subscribing to your account will receive a copy in their inbox.

Subscription

The Subscription button from that menu presents you with videos that you have shown an interest in and might want to subscribe to. This means that whenever the person you have subscribed to posts a new video, you are given notification of that fact.

Click on the Edit Subscription button above the video and set the options as you wish.

Subscription includes:

- ● All videos uploaded, rated, favourited and commented on by daddariostrings
- ○ Only videos uploaded by daddariostrings
- ○ Unsubscribe from daddariostrings
- ☐ Default to this for all future subscriptions
- ☐ Email me for new uploads

[Update] or Cancel

My Videos

This menu option will show all the videos you have uploaded to YouTube. If you right click on the title of the video, you will open a menu option that will offer Send Link which will automatically create an email for you to send to friends to tell them where your latest video can be found.

Backing up your resources

One of the most attractive functions that all of these sites offer is the opportunity to be able to access your materials wherever you are. The resources are stored on some server somewhere, and you can always get at it, and, furthermore, so can your friends and family.

However, it is important to realize that this does not mean that the sites all commit to looking after all your resources and archiving them for you. In fact, Flickr imposes a limit of 200 pictures if you have not paid for the subscription to the site.

So, here are a few suggestions to make sure that you don't lose your creative materials

- Save a copy of your photographs and videos in a folder on your computer. You can use the same structure of sets for both

Madeira	Mair's Birthday
New camera	New Folder
Norfolk 2009	Norfolk Coast Walks
Pembrokeshire	QuickCam
Shetland	South Africa
Sri Lanka 2009	Sri Lanka slide show
Suffolk Coast Walks	Summer 2005

- You can upload materials straight from your camera to YouTube or Flickr. If you then delete the materials from the website, you are in danger of losing the images altogether

- Blogger allows you to export your blog, and the comments your posting has received. Go to Settings, Export Blog is at the top of that page. You can export your blog as a file to save to your hard drive, or, alternatively, save it to post to another blogging tool

Beware

Deleting materials from these websites often removes them permanently. You are usually asked twice before the deletion actually happens.

Following conventions

All the sites we've looked at in this chapter have rules and regulations about what you can upload and display. There are some basic principles that it is worth listing.

- Follow the on-site instructions for content – this will include size of image, length of video, and so on, but it will also discuss the nature of the materials

- All of these sites have the potential to allow people to comment on the resources they find. It is your responsibility, as the content owner, to manage those comments and to ensure that any inappropriate language is removed from the site

- If someone does leave what you consider to be an offensive comment – 'this person can't write' – on your poetry blog, for example, it is best not to become defensive. You can remove their comment, and you might be able to reply to them by email privately. Your best course of action might just be to rise above it, and value the more constructive comments you receive!

- As a site member, do spend some time looking at other people's work, and understanding how they are using the site. That will help you get the most out of it

- When you join other groups – on Flickr for example – there will be rules about how to contribute. Make sure you read them before posting images

In conclusion; all these sites offer places to display your creative talents. If you comment to others as you would like them to comment to you, you will find that you meet new people who become fans of yours, and who can help you develop your creative skills.

10 Using Twitter

This chapter explains how Twitter allows anyone to find out what other people are doing, and it's use by the famous too.

Creating a Twitter account

1 Go to http://twitter.com and select Sign Up

New to Twitter?
Easy, free, and instant updates.
Get access to the information that
interests you most.

Sign Up ›

2 Fill in the form provided. In addition to your own name, email and password, you need to think of a name that you want to be known by. Twitter will check whether it is available

Full name	**Anne Moller**	✔ ok
	Your full name will appear on your public profile	
Username	**Mollerish**	✔ ok
	Your public profile: http://twitter.com/ Mollerish	
Password	••••••	✔ Weak
Email	**anne@themollers.net**	✔ ok

☑ Let others find me by my email address
Note: Email will not be publicly displayed

Terms of Service Printable version

Terms of Service

These Terms of Service ("Terms") govern your access to and use of the services and Twitter's websites (the "Services"), and

By clicking on "Create my account" below, you are agreeing to the Terms of Service above and the Privacy Policy.

Create my account

☑ I want the inside scoop—please send me email updates!

3 Complete the security text to confirm your account, and then confirm your account from email

Are you human?   ✕

Before we create your account, we need to make sure you're not a computer.

505 sevedy

Can't read this?
↻ Get two new words
◀ Hear a set of words
Powered by reCAPTCHA
Help

Type the words above   **505 sevedy**

Finish

Finding the rich and famous

1 A list of topics of interest is provided. Click on one of these to see who is active on Twitter

Art & Design
Books
Business
Charity
Deals & Discounts
Entertainment
Family
Fashion

2 The people who contribute to discussion in that topic area are shown on screen. If you find someone you want to follow, click Follow next to their name

colson whitehead
@colsonwhitehead
Location:
Bio: just another down on his luck carny with a pocketful of broken dreams
follow

Stephen Fry Verified
@stephenfry
Location: London
Bio: British Actor, Writer, Lord of Dance, Prince of Swimwear & Blogger
follow

Bethanne Patrick
@thebookmaven
Location: Arlington, Virginia
Bio: Blogger, book reviewer, author interviewer, author --but above all, a reader.
follow

3 Click on the name after the @ symbol to see a set of the contributions (tweets) that the person has made.

@GrantaMag

4 Listings with this symbol are really the famous person they say they are. Some listings supposedly from a famous person might not be. Some listings are provided by organizations

 Verified

Don't forget

It's going to be unlikely that famous people will write back to you specifically, but they might respond to your Tweet.

Hot tip

Look out for the Twitter names of famous people in the press – sometimes they give them out in interviews.

...cont'd

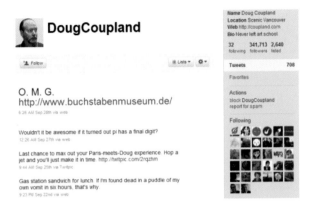

This is characteristic of most Twitter pages. It tells you who owns the page, where they are located, and what their Twitter address is. You can see how many people they follow and how many are following them. The array of photos represent the people who the page owner is following. Rolling your mouse over the picture gives their name. You can see how many tweets the page owner has written, and you can reply or forward it to your followers by choosing Retweet.

It is possible to reply to famous people's tweets. The message will start with the name of the person you have been reading. You then have the balance of 140 characters left to express yourself. Here there are 129 characters left.

Hot tip

Visit the official website of the celebrity you are interested in. They often give information about their social networking links.

Finding people you know

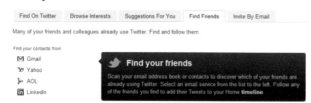

See if your friends are on Twitter

| Find On Twitter | Browse Interests | Suggestions For You | Find Friends | Invite By Email |

Many of your friends and colleagues already use Twitter. Find and follow them.

Find your contacts from

M Gmail
Y! Yahoo
AOL
in LinkedIn

🐦 **Find your friends**

Scan your email address book or contacts to discover which of your friends are already using Twitter. Select an email service from the list to the left. Follow any of the friends you find to add their Tweets to your Home **timeline**.

1 Go to the Find People option from the top menu

2 You can search for a specific person using Find on Twitter

3 Using Find Friends, you can access your email contacts on Gmail, Yahoo or AOL, and also contacts you might have on LinkedIn

4 Whichever way you find contacts, they will be provided in a list and you can choose to follow them or not

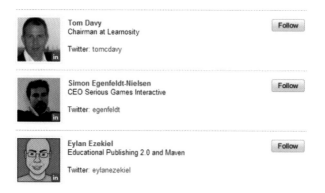

5 When Twitter finds you have friends who are not yet using Twitter, it offers you the opportunity to invite them

179

Your profile

Creating your profile is a straightforward process. Go to Settings to change the way Twitter looks – the Profile tab takes you to your page of Tweets, and the presentation of information for others. To change the profile content, go to settings.

Account Information

● This gives your name and Twitter username

● You can also see your email address and decide whether or not other people can search for your email address

● You can set the language that you Twitter in – English is the default, but there are a few others available

● You are asked to choose the timezone you are in

● If you are in America, you can decide whether other users can see your location when they read your tweets. This location can be very precise, so think carefully if you want people to be able to work out your home address, and, perhaps more worryingly, that you're not at your home address

● Tweet Privacy is also set here. It offers you the opportunity to approve people who will follow you

When you have set this information, you need to select Save.

Password

The next tab allows you to reset your password.

Mobile

This tab controls your mobile phone access. (We'll discuss this further in chapter 12)

Notices

This section provides text boxes where you can decide to receive emails when you have a new follower, when you get a new direct message, and if there is an email update.

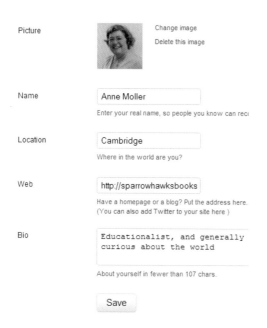

Picture — Change image / Delete this image

Name — Anne Moller
Enter your real name, so people you know can rec

Location — Cambridge
Where in the world are you?

Web — http://sparrowhawksbooks
Have a homepage or a blog? Put the address here.
(You can also add Twitter to your site here.)

Bio — Educationalist, and generally curious about the world
About yourself in fewer than 107 chars.

Save

Don't forget

Brevity is really valued in the world of Twitter. Be concise in your description.

The content of this page is important as it will have some impact on whether you can be found by other people. A lot of use of Twitter is to find out what other people are doing, and to share your activities with them too.

Some Korean researchers found that Twitter was the fastest way of spreading information, and that is because the networks and links people make on Twitter are not reciprocal. It's not about two people sharing information between themselves, it's about one person having the potential to pass information on to many, and the next layer out to do the same. So that is why setting up your profile so that it interests others is important. A photograph is really helpful, as is a few words of biography.

Design

This final settings section allows you to decide how the background of your page will look. You can change both the background image and also the background colors.

Don't forget

Twitter was also in the news during the recent Iranian election. It was a fantastic way for people outside Iran to find out what was going on, and for people in Iran to get support from others.

Posting tweets

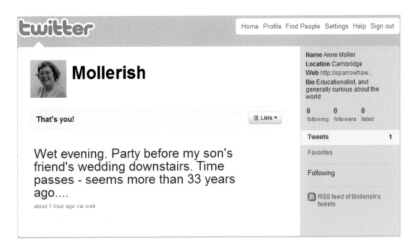

This is typical of a lot of tweets. It's answering the question, "what's happening". To be honest, a lot of these sorts of tweets are fairly inconsequential and not of real interest to me. They do not have to be like that, however, and as you spend a bit of time exploring the site, you'll begin to find people that you want to reply to, or comments that make you think about something you want to say.

As well as finding people to follow, another way of finding people to communicate with is by searching for a topic. Find the search box on the home page and enter a search term for a topic that interests you.

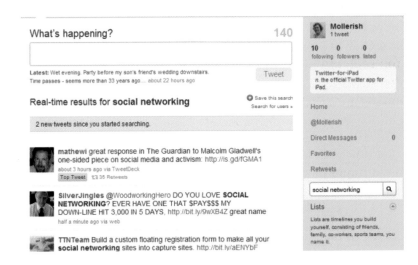

The search on Social Networking has thrown up a large number of tweets, a few of which are shown on the first page. Click More at the bottom of the page to see another batch.

There are some conventions in creating tweets that you need to know.

tweetersname
The name of the person posting the tweet appears at the beginning of the message in bold.

@tweetersname
The @ symbol tells you that they have been reading a tweet by the person named, and that this tweet is in part a response to it.

http://bit.ly/fGMA1
This is a shortened link to a website that they want to refer you to (How to do this, is described on page 185). Shortening website links is essential for Twitter, as a full link address might use up all your 140 characters!

Recycling symbol
You can see this next to the "Top Tweet" tag on the first tweet opposite. This means that the person has retweeted this message to 35 people.

Hash tags
You sometimes see these "#" symbols in messages. Include the # symbol if you are contributing to a topic that lots of others are writing about. You can search #politics to find political tweets, for example.

Don't forget

Searching for topics that you are interested in. Including the # in the search term might help you find many tweets that are about the topic that interests you.

...cont'd

Your first tweet

This can be on any topic. If it's not linked to something, you will probably find that it is not picked up on or replied to by anyone. You must fit the entire message into 140 characters, including any web site links you include.

Replying to a tweet

Replying to a tweet goes directly to the person who posted the tweet, and it can also be seen by all of your followers, and all of the followers of the person you addressed it to.

To reply, click on the reply arrow on the tweet, and the @ followed by the person's tweet name will be added automatically into your text box. As you will see from the image above, there were 11 more characters that I could have sent in my reply. When my reply appears as a tweet on my home page (and on the page of the person I've sent it to), there is a link that shows what prompted my comment.

Retweeting

Select Retweet and the recycle symbol from a tweet allows you to choose to send it on to your followers. This feature has revolutionized Twitter and has enabled it to ensure that messages travel really quickly through the community.

...cont'd

Private messages

You can send a private message to someone who is following you. You cannot send a private message to anyone else. Go to the follower's Profile page and find the actions section on the right hand tool bar (just above the pictures of those following that person). Click on the word message, and a box will open for you to write your tweet to them in.

Don't forget

You can only send a private message to someone who is a follower of you.

Shortening website addresses

There are a number of websites that offer this service, but the one that is probably used by most people on Twitter is http://bit.ly. It lets you take a long link to a particular article at a newspaper, for example, and then shorten it to a handful of characters.

Copy the link from your browser and paste it into the top text box. Select Shorten and the link that you then want is provided in the green text box. A similar service is provided by www.tinyurl.com and also www.is.gd.

It is possible to sign up for these services rather than just use them as a one off link. Their full service offers web link analysis as well.

Beware

These shortened addresses give you no clues about where you are going to go. Some Twitter users might take you to sites that you consider inappropriate.

Other Twitter features

Marking a favorite

Sometimes it is really useful to be able to save a tweet, so that you can find it again to refer to. There have been people who have attended conferences and tweeted links to information about what is happening so that their followers can share. You might then want to find that saved information at a future date, and one way you can do this is by marking a tweet as a favorite.

There is a star on the top right of the tweet. Click on this to mark it for your favorite list.

Don't forget

You can protect your tweets, if you want, by selecting 'Protect my tweets'. This will limit your activity on Twitter considerably, and will make it a very sterile experience.

When you then click on Favorites from your menu on the home page, you will be able to find it easily.

@yourusername

When you have been actively using Twitter for a while, there are likely to be people who have been referring to you, or who have replied to your tweets. Messages where you have been referred to in this way can be found by clicking on @yourusername on the menu on the homepage.

Hot tip

Finding out who has been replying to your tweets is both interesting and gives you the list of their followers, who are people that you might want to link to directly.

Retweets

Selecting Retweets from the menu on the homepage provides a link to show you who you have retweeted, and also who has retweeted the tweets you have posted.

TopTweets

Sometimes you see this message posted on a tweet. That is because lots of people have been retweeting it or commenting on it.

Lists

Lists are a way of organizing users into groups or "lists". When you have created a list, you will see all the tweets from the people in that list. You can put users into a list that you are not actually following. That means that their posts will not normally appear on your home page or timeline, but, when you open the list with them in, you will be able to see all the posts that they have made (interspersed with the others in that list).

Some Twitter users make their lists available to the community to subscribe to. This is a very easy way of finding out what is going on, and building on the expertise of someone else in the community.

Don't forget

You are allowed to have up to twenty different lists at any one time, and up to 500 accounts on each list.

1. Visit the profile of the first person you want to add to your list and then click on this icon

2. At the bottom of the drop down menu, select Create a list

3. Give the list a name and brief description. Decide whether others can subscribe to the list

Hot tip

You can add users from anywhere you see the drop down list icon on someone's profile. Check the box for the list you want to include them in.

4. Make sure that the Twitter user you wanted has been included in your list - a blue tick will be next to the list, which you will find by clicking on the List drop-down icon (next to No1 in these instructions)

Twitpics

Twitter has made its name by only supporting messages of 140 characters or less, so perhaps it seems a little surprising that it has links with a site that allows users to post pictures. This is called twitpic and can be accessed by going to www.twitpic.com.

1 Select Login or Create an Account on twitpic

2 This asks you to confirm that you would like to link via Twitter – click Allow

3 Choose your photo and add a message. Then choose upload, to post the photo to Twitter. This may take some time depending on the size of the photo

4 You can view the photo in Twitpic and then go back to Twitter. You will find that a link to your photo has been included in the message you have created

Hot tip

This service is useful for creating links to photographs that you can use in emails too.

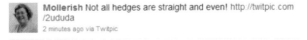

Mollerish Not all hedges are straight and even! http://twitpic.com /2ududa
2 minutes ago via Twitpic

11 Using Meetup

Creating real–world social events using Meet Up is described in this chapter.

Using Meetup to find groups

You can explore a lot of the features of Meetup without joining and logging in. So you can wait to log in until you have decided to join a group, if you want. The home page offers you two boxes to enter – a topic of interest to you and a City or Zip code. Fundamental to the purpose of Meetup is that its users want to physically meet. So, if you find just the group that you are interested in joining, but in a different country or many miles away, then your options are either to start a group yourself, or to find something else to do locally.

Don't forget

Have a good look around the site to get a feel for the sort of groups that exist, and which you might want to join.

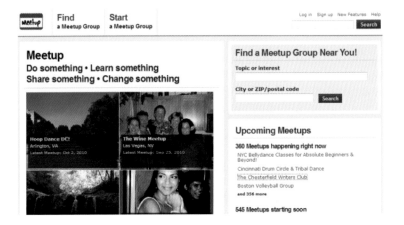

You can use the home page to get a sense of what is going on currently – all over the world, including the US, UK and India. There's a vast range of activities too, some with a serious purpose, and others with a much more social focus.

Find a Meetup Group

There's a vast range of different activities available, but, if your interest is rather esoteric, it might be frustrating to find that there are no like-minded people within your local area. Of course, they may be there waiting for you to create and arrange a meetup to get them out of the woodwork. For the purposes of exploring the functions of this site, let us suppose that we are mandolin players and are interested in meeting up with other instrumentalists for a jam session. If you type your interest into the Topic text box, you will

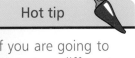

Hot tip

If you are going to move to a different location, or visit a new country for a while, Meetup can be a great way of finding new friends.

...cont'd

get the events that you could join, their dates and general location.

This panel shows you the range of events happening, and you can use the arrows on the right and left of the group to check through to the next group of events. If you scroll a little further down the page, you can find a brief summary of the groups and some details of the event being planned.

Selecting the name of the group takes you to their Group page. The color and precise design of their group page will vary, but the basic layout and content of the page is fairly standard, with these sections generally available.

The sign up process is the same – you need to join Meetup in order to join a Group. You can also choose to join using your Facebook account.

Don't forget

These panels only show the events happening, either now or very soon.

191

Hot tip

Joining from a group's page gets you straight into one group. If you think you might want to join others, join Meetup on the Home page.

Creating your Meetup account

Whether you choose to join a group directly, or select 'Sign Up' from the home page, you will be asked to give your name, email address and password.

Sign up

Meetup members, Log in

Your real name

Anne Sparrowhawk

Your email

anne@somewhere.com

We hate spam too. We won't share your address!

Pick a password

••••••

Sign up

— OR —

Join this Meetup Group even quicker with your Facebook account.

f Sign up using Facebook

By clicking the "Sign up using Facebook" or "Sign up" buttons above, you agree to Meetup's Terms of Service

If you choose to connect via your Facebook account, then you are not asked for any further information – Facebook provides it to Meetup directly.

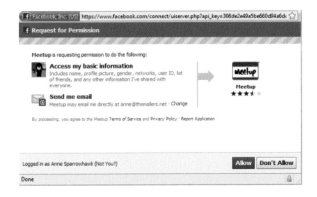

...cont'd

For either route, you are next presented with the following message. The Terms of Service are accessible from this message too.

If you have joined up via a Group, the first thing you will be asked for is a bit of background about yourself. I've signed up to join a mandolin group, so I'm asked for some introductory information, and some questions that are specific to this group – what instruments I play, what level of experience I have, and whether I sing.

The introduction you write to a group profile can be specific to that group. You have the opportunity to write something different about yourself each time you join a group, which is logical really. My mandolin playing friends might not be interested in what books I like to read, or that I go walking at the weekends. This form also allows you to choose whether to have emails directly from group members or only from the official group organizer.

Don't forget

If the group you have joined is an active one, there might be lots of emails – choosing 'one daily email' might be a sensible starting option.

...cont'd

If you join Meetup without identifying a particular group to join, you are given a form through which to express your interest in topics that you are interested in. In the example below, the location of Saratoga Springs as a starting point has been deduced from searches that had been done in Meetup.

The tool to the left of the screen allows you to select topics that you are interested in and about, Meetup will email you when there's a relevant group in your area. You can also indicate how far you would be prepared to travel. Click on one of the broader categories here to produce a subset of topics from which you can choose.

Hot tip

Choose a number of different topics so that you find out about the range of things Meetup does. You don't have to join all the groups at once.

Explore Meetup

What do you want to meet about near Saratoga Springs?
Add topics to your list and **we'll email** you as soon as someone starts a new Meetup Group!

We'll email you about:

We'll email you about:

Genetics

Life Sciences

Biology

Archaeology

Medieval History

History

Natural Learning

Internet Professionals

Work At Home

Select a category below to see topics.

Arts & Entertainment	Business & Career
Cultures & Languages	Communities & Lifestyles
Internet & Technology	Health & Support
Politics & Activism	Hobbies
Science	Parenting & Family
Sports & Recreation	Pets & Animals
	Religion & Beliefs
	Social
	Education

Or start typing to find a topic:

How far would you travel for a Meetup?
○ 5 miles ○ 10 miles ○ 25 miles ● 50 miles ○ 100 miles

save

Don't forget

There are lots of layers of topics underneath these main categories. Explore different layers to find new topics of interest.

The list on the left of this image has been developed by moving through the various topics offered and selecting those that might be potentially interesting to me. As you can see, they are still quite broad as topics go. Remember to select Save when you have finished making your choices.

Editing your account details

1 Select 'Account' from the top menu bar

Don't forget

People will actually get to meet you, so it would be best if your photo looked like you!

2 The 'Personal Info' section allows you to edit the location, as well as the basic identification elements of your account. The 'Bio' you enter here can be general biographical details - you add in more personal details when you join a specific group. You can set which links to other networking sites appear on your Meetup Group profiles. If you have not set the topics you are interested in when you joined, you always have an opportunity to set them here

Hot tip

Having all your different social networks linked together can make it easier to keep each of the accounts filled with current information.

...cont'd

Don't forget

Make sure you click on Save when you have made any changes to your profile.

3 The next section of the Account details tells you which groups you belong to, and sets your privacy for the site. You can choose to be contacted by any member of Meetup, members of your groups, or only organizers and their assistants

4 The next section of Membership and Communication defines who can email you and, therefore, how often that communication might be. This is a setting for Meetup overall, not just your Group. You can also arrange to have SMS messages sent to your mobile

Hot tip

It can be difficult to make sure you get enough information, but not too much. It's easy to adjust the levels later.

5 The 'Payments Made' section helps you to manage any dues or subs that you might have to pay to join events

6 'Meetup API' is a section that allows you access to communicate with the web site from your mobile phone, or gives you tools to use to create your own Group, if you so wish

Attending events

1 When you've found the group you want to join, go to this menu item and select either Upcoming (for their next meeting) or Calendar for one slightly further off

2 The event you are interested in will have an RSVP button next to it. Select this to indicate your attendance. As a member of the group, it is polite to indicate that you won't be coming, too. If you want to bring a guest, you will be asked details here

3 You will see that your response has been added to the list on the right of the screen

4 If you've linked your response to another social networking site, you'll be asked if you want to make the link active

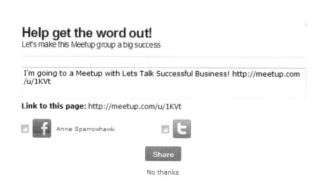

197

...cont'd

5 You can print a ticket for the event, which provides a map as well as the event agenda

Lets Talk Successful Business Monthly Meetup
Export to a calendar | Print ticket

Lets Talk Successful Business Monthly Meetup

Tuesday, October 5, 2010 6:15 PM
Lets Talk Successful Business

Black Horse House
Castle Park, Cambridge.
07802 433988

Meetup agenda:
Lets Talk Successful Business
will be held on 1st Tuesday
each month, starting
1/12/2009.
Timings are 6.15pm to 8.30pm.

The venue is Lloyds TSB
Commercial Area Directors
Office Black Horse House

6 Make sure you have added your group profile information before you attend the event

7 Some meetings are more photogenic than others! Members are encouraged to upload photos of events. Click on the name of the photo album for the event to access the Add photos button and the link to your computer's pictures

Meetup
Add photos

8 Add a review of the event. Go to the Meetups menu, Review is the bottom button. You have to have attended the event to write a review!

Great hike with vivid red, yellow and orange foliage set against deep blue skies. Fun surprise seeing the flock of wild turkey enroute. I especially enjoyed hiking in the company of nice people. Thank you MaryJoy for organizing and hosting such a wonderful outing!

— Roxanne

Creating your own group

If you are going to organize your own group and plan and run events, you will need to subscribe to Meetup. It charges a monthly subscription fee, but guarantees to pay it back if the use of Meetup does not work out for you within 30 days.

Meetup provides a basic concept overview that you need to understand as a Group Organizer.

Setting your country and zip code will prompt Meetup to suggest some location based names for your group – Cambridge Creatives, for example. Similarly, clicking into the Group description text box will prompt a flyout box suggesting what you should include in the description.

You are asked to define what your members are called and then to create an appropriate web name to follow meetup. com. Finally, you have to commit to pledge to create a real face-to-face community.

As you complete each of these elements, you will see the impact of your changes on a preview area to the right.

When you select 'Submit', you move on to the next step in the process, which is to design what the page is going to look like. First you get to choose the color and background setting for your group. As you do so, you can see a preview of what the screen will look like. You can try as many as you like before you decide. You can also design your own.

Hot tip

You have 5000 characters to describe your group. Look at other groups and see what they have done. Some are explicit about they type of membership they are seeking, and also who the group is NOT for.

Don't forget

You can see how your Group page is going to look in the panel on the right.

...cont'd

Hot tip

Choose topics that define your group, but don't make it up to 15 topics if they are not all relevant.

Topics are a common feature of all groups. Each group has a panel defining the topics they see themselves as exploring. Selecting the topics your group is interested in is important, both for your group page, but also as a way of driving potential group members to you. As you type the first group into the template, related groups will appear on the right of the screen. You can choose from these. Up to 15 topics can be chosen for your group.

Beware

As with many website subscriptions, the site automatically renews. So, if you've paid for 6 months and then find you are not using it, remember to cancel the credit card payment.

The next step in the process is to pay your subscription. The charge is in dollars and is cheapest if paid as a 6 month subscription.

Once you have paid, you are invited to decide whether your group has a message board, and/or a mailing list. You can also write a welcome email for new members, and set any specific questions you want to have answered by all new members when they join.

Message boards like this allow you members to ask questions that are relevant to your group, and to share information that might support and aid group members.

Creating your first event

It's much easier to get other people to join a group if there is at least one event planned. This is a list of the basic elements of the plan you need to have got underway.

- Select 'Group Tools' from your group's toolbar and select 'Schedule a Meetup' from the drop-down menu

- The basics: Create a title, date, and description of your event, and specify who's responsible for organizing it

- Where is it?: Choose a location from 'Your Venue,' or 'Find a Meetup Venue,' or click 'Add a new Venue' to select a brand new venue

- Charging for this Meetup?: You'll need to decide what you are charging for the event, and indicate the fees here. You will need to select a payment method for your Members and include a refund policy

- RSVP Settings: If the venue can only accommodate a certain number of people, you will need to limit the attendees here. You can enable a Waiting List so that others can take up vacated places

- Email Settings: Enable or disable automatic reminders for you and your Members

- Ask questions when Members RSVP: You can ask up to 10 questions that Members answer when they RSVP

- Promote this Meetup: Select whether or not to promote your event on Facebook or other social networks

When you've filled in these details, click 'Schedule this Meetup Now' to add it to the group Calendar. You can save it as a draft if you have not completely finalized the event. The event will then be saved without being published to the Calendar.

The event then appears on the Meetup calendar and can be seen by people in the area, or by those searching for that topic.

Don't forget

If you ask too many questions when members join, they might be put off!

...cont'd

Your role as group organizer

You can set the rules for how the group will operate, and it's important that these are published and clear for new users. Many groups put this sort of information on their home page, and some add specific policies that group members agree to adhere to by joining.

Hot tip

Find someone else to work with as you set up the group. Make sure the rules are written clearly, but not officiously.

Table of Contents		
Page title	**Most recent update**	**Last edited by**
Policies	July 21, 2010 9:53 AM	Jason
Rating System	July 21, 2010 9:56 AM	Jason
About Hiking Mates of the Capital Region	September 8, 2010 1:49 PM	Jason

One of the other activities that only the organizer can do is set up photo albums. Photos are very actively shared in some groups, so making sure that the album for an event is available immediately after the event will encourage users to take part.

Managing the money

Some people charge a small fee to join the Group. This can have the effect of putting some people off joining. On the other hand, it can have the effect of making people make a positive choice to join and then to attend events regularly.

Whether you have to make sure that people pay for events is down to the sort of group you are. If you hire a hall, for example, then you will be likely to incur that cost whether the event has attendees or not. If you are a walking group, then perhaps it does not matter whether 10 or 15 people turn up for the walk.

Some groups charge a nominal sum for a meetup, which the organizer can put towards the monthly Meetup subscription costs.

There are a number of different ways in which you can arrange for payments. Of course, cash at meetings is a very straightforward way of taking the money from group

Don't forget

Listen carefully to the expectations that the group members have about how much things should cost to do.

members. Alternatively, you can arrange a PayPal account (www.paypal.com) group members can use to make credit card payments into, and which you can then transfer to a regular bank account.

If you are in the USA, you can also use payments.amazon.com as a way to collect money.

Both of these mechanisms make transaction fees.

Connecting PayPal to Meetup

1 Connect your PayPal account to your Meetup account by going to the 'Payments Received' section of your group account page

2 Under 'Your PayPal account' enter your PayPal email address. Agree to the Meetup 'Terms of Service' and click 'Submit'

Each group can only have one PayPal account related to it.

There is an account management tool built into Meetup that allows you to see which of your group members has paid and also to manage your expenses.

For the advanced Meetup organizer

The New Features menu on the top of the Meetup tool bar offers access to a whole range of features and tools that can be used to make your group's experience of Meetup richer. There are lots of different tools to do with how you present information on the site, being able to include video or share photographs between Facebook and Twitter with Meetup, for example.

Don't forget

Managing the accounts needs to be transparent, so that everyone feels the group is being run fairly.

Beware

Make sure you don't spend so much time adding the latest new gizmo to your group's pages that you forget to meet face-to-face!

Meetup Everywhere

Meetups are intended to be face-to-face meetings. But there are lots of groups of people around the Meetup world who share common interests and concerns. Meetup Everywhere is for them. It is intended to support a cause or a brand, a writer or a TV show. It might draw members from anywhere across the world, and draw a lot of value from people in other countries, where experiences have been different.

The intention is that, by having an overarching Meetup tool, people can mobilize and organize groups in many different locations comparing and sharing experiences.

Hot tip

If you want to run a campaign but not get involved in meeting people, then this is not the right place for you to do that – you'd be better off with a Facebook page.

1 To find out about Meetup Everywhere, go to www.meetup.com/everywhere

2 To access a Meetup Everywhere event, select one of the topics that you find interesting. It will show you where meetup interest is, and enables you to join in an event

3 To create your own Meetup Everywhere topic, go to Get Started and complete the template that it offers. You don't have to have a paid for account to do this

12 Your Phone and Social Networking

Keeping connected to your social networks while you are out and about is now possible and exciting, as will be discussed in this chapter.

Things to think about

All the services that we've been talking about in this book are all based on the Internet. As Smartphones and iPhones offer connectivity to the Internet when you are out and about, it becomes possible to access some of these sites from your phone. Of all the sites, Twitter is probably the one that benefits most from this facility. It allows people who are at conferences, or an exciting exhibition or sporting event, to communicate directly with others via the Internet.

Via Twitter

From English swimmer Liam Tancock on Twitter: "Really pleased with my first day of racing at the Commonwealth Games."

Tancock helped England to men's 4x100m freestyle silver, and qualified for Tuesday's 50m backstroke final too.

Not only are journalists now using Twitter to send stories back home, but competitors are too.

One of the challenges of this new technology is getting the balance right. When you are out and about, you perhaps should not be looking constantly at the mobile – and certainly not when walking along the street or driving. However, whilst you wait for the train, a friend to arrive at the café, or your grandson to come out of school, a little social networking might not be a problem.

The concepts

Using your phone to interact with social networking sites has a number of implications about it.

- It assumes that you can see and read what other people have been putting either on your page or on theirs

- It also assumes that you can contribute content to the site in response

- Both of these actions require a telephone or wireless connection to be in place, and, in both cases, the time the information takes to upload will depend on the speed and efficiency of your connection

- Mobile phone connectivity often still carries a cost that is dependent on the amount you use it, so do bear that in mind when you access your social networking sites

- There has to be a link set up between the mobile phone and your account. This usually happens because there is a piece of software downloaded onto your phone – an App (short for Application). This is the program that does the work, translating what is happening on the Internet into a form that your phone can display, and back again. Most social networking sites have such programs, and this chapter will explain what you need to do to access them

- Your mobile phone has to know your account details so that it can put your information in the right place. This requires a complex checking process to make sure that the person with the phone has the right to update the website. Usually, this requires accessing emails to start the phone connection working

- Not all the services allow you to do all the different things you can do with the site when you are at a computer. Make sure you know what the limitations are, so that you don't rely on doing something that actually won't be possible

- Increasingly, social networking sites are using the location information that is provided automatically by phone. There are situations when you might not want everyone to know that you are on holiday, or at a particular location. There are settings that allow you to override this location feature on some services

There is no reason why you have to use your phone on all of your social networking services. Perhaps the best way forward is to try one or two, and find out how you get on, and then add services when you think you 'need' them.

Hot tip

If you know you are going to want to make an account work from a phone, set it up and check that it's working while you have use of a computer, before you rely on the phone when you are out.

Beware

If you use your phone when you are abroad, many of these services become extremely expensive. Turn off Roaming after you have used it.

Using Hootsuite

Hootsuite is a service that allows you to communicate with several of your social networks through a single interface. You can read recent inputs to your different accounts on one screen, and manage them all without having to go to their individual websites. It is particularly useful if you want to schedule status information - as you can prepare it beforehand, and then have the messages posted as you have determined.

Hot tip

You need to be an active user of at least two social networks to make Hootsuite worthwhile.

 1 To sign up for this service, go to www.hootsuite.com

2 Complete the login information required

3 You will arrive at the screen below

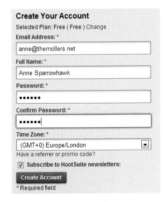

4 You need to carry out the linking up process for each of the social networks you want to connect. Select Allow

5 The process that you follow for each site is the same. You will be asked to confirm that you want the link to be made

6 Select the next network you want to link to from the top of the screen, below where it says 'Add Social Network'

209

Don't forget

The screens each service asks you to complete to establish the link might look slightly different, but the principles will be the same.

7 Choose how you would like the program to look on your desktop, from the options offered using the radio button

Don't forget

You can come and change the look later if you find the colorway you have chosen difficult to use.

...cont'd

Hot tip

If you have included Twitter in this site, you will need to keep your status messages to less than 140 characters, so watch the counter.

Hootsuite's features

- Click on the owl at the top left to activate your account

- The profile icons on the top right indicate the accounts for the different social networks you have included. If you have a different profile picture in each social network, it will make it easier to use Hootsuite

- Click on the profile icons to ensure that the message you want to send gets sent to each of the sites

- Click on the message bar to write a message. It counts the 140 characters that Twitter allows you, and the larger number that Facebook allows too

Hot tip

Try using the scheduler to send a message in 10 minutes time. Then you can see how it works.

- Put a web address in the text box at the bottom, and select Shrink to reduce it for inclusion in Twitter

- Select the Calendar (icon with 30 on it) to schedule when you would like your message to be posted. Select the floppy disc icon to save the draft message for later dispatch

- Use the Send now button to send the message to all of your chosen social networks

Facebook

1 To set up your mobile phone with Facebook, go to the Account menu and select Mobile

2 Select the link to Facebook Mobile

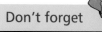

Don't forget

Think about what you use Facebook for, to help you decide which way you want to connect to it from your phone.

More Facebook Mobile products

Upload via email

Use a personalised upload email address to post status updates or send photos and videos straight to your profile. Your personal email address is:

Send my upload email to me now

Find out more

facebook.com

- Update your status, browse your News Feed and view friends' Profiles all from your phone.
- Works on all phones with mobile web access.

Text a link to my phone

Facebook for your phone

Download rich, interactive applications built for your phone. Available for:

iPhone   Nokia
Palm   Android
Sony Ericsson   Windows Mobile
INQ   Sidekick
Blackberry

3 There are three different services described here. The 'Upload via email' provides you with a unique email address to which you can post photos and information from your phone. Facebook.com offers a fuller experience of the site. Downloading the product for the phone is provided for a range of different phones. It is a relatively new service, and some further development is almost inevitable

4 Choose which service you want. In each case, click on the blue text under the image to open up a window where you can enter information about your phone, followed by a phone number to which it will be sent. Instructions will be provided on your phone if there is an installation process to follow

Hot tip

Lots of phones now enable you to have Facebook on your home screen for your phone. You will be logged straight in, ready for use.

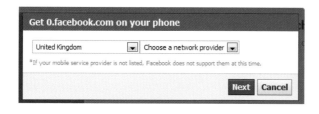

Get 0.facebook.com on your phone

| United Kingdom ▼ | Choose a network provider ▼ |

*If your mobile service provider is not listed, Facebook does not support them at this time.

Next   Cancel

MySpace

MySpace offers a simple service to its mobile users – it provides a specific web address that is unique to you. You can use this to send an email and you can either send picture messages from your phone (MMS) or emails to the address given.

Hot tip

Copy your MySpace email address to your email account. Send an email to yourself at the email account you use on your mobile. You can then copy that to the mobile's address book.

1 To find your email link, go to 'My Account' and select Mobile

2 This will open a page which will give you your unique email address. It is long: You can either enter it directly into your phone or, alternatively, use your email service to send it to yourself

Send Photos From Your Phone

Send your photos to : ▓▓▓▓▓▓▓▓▓▓▓m

You can send picture messages (MMS) or emails to this address, and attached photos will be automatically uploaded to your My Mobile Photos folder. Please do not share this email address with others.

> [Change Upload Email] [Disable Upload Email]

Upload Limit Per Day : 250

> [Save All Changes]

3 If you need to disable the upload email – perhaps someone else has copied the address – you can also come back to this page and get issued with a new email address

LinkedIn

LinkedIn

The easiest place to find the link to LinkedIn's mobile solutions is in the footer of any page. Click Mobile for a page where you can find out about resources available for your phone.

Currently, LinkedIn supports the iPhone, BlackBerry and Palm, with applications designed to be downloaded for installation on the phone.

For any other phone, you need to go to the following address: http://m.linkedin.com from the browser on your phone. The image below on the left shows the iPhone interface, and the one on the right, the basic search tools offered to phones without full LinkedIn applications as yet.

Hot tip

Use LinkedIn on your mobile when you want to find someone's contact details.

Blogger

Blogger.com allows you to post text and photos to its blog site, but not directly to your own post. Instead, it publishes the post as a new blog and tells you where you can find it. This is a service that is currently only available in the US.

Beware

You need to have set this up from your computer before you want to use it – don't try to set it up just from your phone.

1 First send a text message from your mobile phone.
To: BLOGGR
Message: REGISTER

2 You will then get a message back with the address of the mobile blog, together with a code to claim that address as yours

3 Enter the claim token and Captcha code

Hot tip

Since Blogger automatically puts all your mobile blogs in one place, it can be a simple way of compiling a travel diary while you're on the go.

4 You can then send text and pictures to your mobile blog. Once you have set it up, any blog that you post from your mobile will go to the same blog

5 If you want to, you can merge the mobile blog with your existing blog. To do this, go to go.blogger.com and enter the token that was sent to your phone

6 Text UNREGISTER to BLOGGR to stop blogging from your phone

Flickr

You can access your Flickr account to share with someone via your mobile phone. To do this, log in to http://m.flickr.com. You can then access your own account by typing in your login and password. You can show people your flickr albums and explore other people's photos too – a general experience that is not unlike browsing Flickr at a computer, though the interface is much simpler

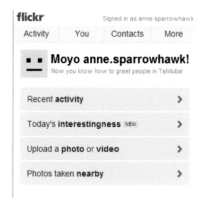

If you want to upload images to Flickr, you need to visit the Flickr mobile website first.

1 Go to http://m.flickr.com and click 'More' on the menu above

2 You will then see an option for 'Upload'. Click on that

3 You will be given a unique email address to which you should upload your photographs. The subject line of the email will be used as the title of the photo, and the body of the email will be used as the description

4 If you want to add tags to the photo, you can do that by adding a new line to the body text
tags: Fred "Mary Scott"

Hot tip

If you want to set the photos you upload as visible to friends and family only, use the following address yourprivatecode+ff@ photos.flickr.com

YouTube

YouTube was probably one of the first sites to really recognize the full potential of being able to use a mobile phone to access videos, and also to upload videos you've taken with your phone.

To watch videos from YouTube

All you need to do to watch videos on a phone is to go to the usual address www.youtube.com and then select the video you want to watch. You can access your account too, by logging in the usual way.

To upload videos from your phone to YouTube

1 Log on to your YouTube account

2 Select 'Upload' from the top menu bar. When the page opens, just underneath Upload is a link to YouTube direct mobile. Click 'Set Up'

| Upload | annesparrowhawk ▼ | Sign Out |

YouTube direct mobile uploads
Did you know that you can upload directly
from your mobile phone?
Set up | Learn more

3 You will be given an email address that is specific to you. Enter this address into your email account on your mobile phone

4 Take the video and then send it to the email address YouTube has given you. It will then show you that it is uploading

5 Next time you access YouTube on your computer, you can edit the detail around the video, but it will be there, already waiting for you

Beware

Make sure you have an unlimited data plan for your phone before you start accessing and posting videos. It can be very expensive if you do not.

Don't forget

You'll need to go back to the videos you've uploaded from your phone to add all the detail about them when you are next at a computer online.

Twitter

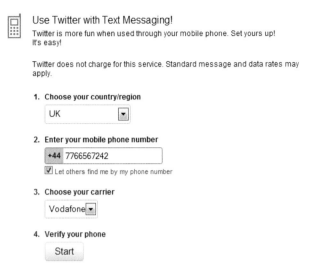

This is the interface that comes up on your Twitter account when you choose Mobile from the Settings menu. It allows you to check that your phone will work with Twitter. Sometimes it needs to have an application available, which has been pre-loaded by the phone company. Sometimes you will need to activate it from the phone.

When you open the application, you might not need to log in every time. You will be able to see your Home and have the text box at the top ready for you to tweet.

You can also choose to have text messages sent to your mobile by clicking on the phone icon on the profile page of anyone you are following.

Don't forget

You can include web links in your tweets, even if you are sending them from a mobile phone.

Meetup

There are a number of applications available to enable phone users to access their Meetup account information. These are still developing, and reviews on the Internet indicate that some experiences are easier and smoother than others. What is available to you will depend on where you are and what phone you own.

1 To find out about the applications available, go to your Meetup account and choose 'Account' from the top menu and then Meetup API

2 Select the 'Learn more about ...' link and choose Applications

3 There are a number of different applications identified here that may suit your phone. Follow the instructions on screen to activate. The experiences they offer will vary and, in some instances, they are more about uploading images to the site than managing the account

Visual
Glossary

What does it look like?

One of the interesting challenges of getting to grips with a new area of computing is the jargon, which is sometimes used by those in the know to baffle and confuse the rest. This section is all about giving you an understanding of what the feature you have been directed to use might actually look like. Of course, there are many different examples of the specific elements within this list, and the visual image chosen has got some design features that have made it fit within the layout of the site it belongs to. However, the picture included should help you recognize what is being discussed or referred to from the text or discussed in the media.

blog
A way to publish text and pictures on the Internet.

breadcrumb trail
A way to show you how the files are structured, and your path to the current screen.

captcha
A process for computers to check that humans are logging onto computer sites, not other computers.

chat

A sequence of text messages that are a conversation between people on a networking site - sometimes one to one, and sometimes one to many.

comment

A public response to someone's material on a social networking site.

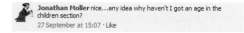

digest

A daily, weekly or monthly update of what's been happening on one of your social networks, from your point of view.

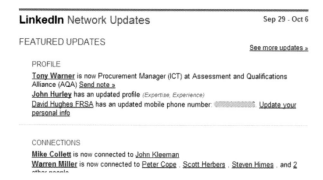

drop-down menu

A menu that opens out to show the options when you click on the top menu bar.

follower

A person who subscribes to the updates of someone who writes on Twitter, and who is represented by an image here.

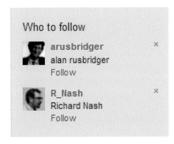

forum

An online space where people can discuss subjects on which they share an interest.

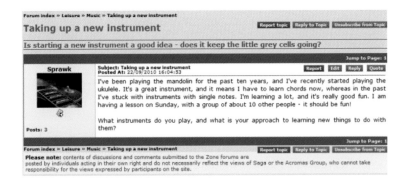

friend request

A request by someone to become a friend on the network you both belong to.

flyout

A menu that extends away from the place that you clicked to open it.

group

A number of members of a social network who regularly communicate about a topic of shared interest.

Home

The main screen of a site, which comes up when you first log on.

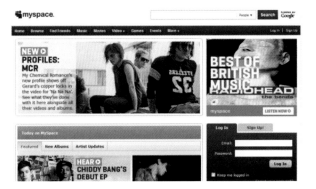

(Hyper)link

A place on a website that, when you click on it, takes you to another part of that website, or somewhere else entirely.

New and the arrow next to it, and the menu items are Hyperlinks

icon

A graphic that represents something on a website; it might, for example, represent a section of the site, a person, or an activity.

login

The process of telling the website that you want to visit who you are – usually with a name or email address and a password, which, in combination, are unique to you.

message

Messages are usually direct communications between two users of a social network, and so cannot be read by other people.

moderation

The process of managing comments left on a website that you have some responsibility for – you might be a group administrator, for example. It is designed to make sure that messages that are left are appropriate.

40. At 9:54pm on 06 Oct 2010, **micktug** wrote:

This comment was removed because the moderators found it broke the House Rules.

navigation bar

This is the correct technical term for the control bar that is at the top of most social networking websites, and which offers access to the main controls for the site.

password

A set of letters or numbers in a combination that allows you to access your own page of a site. It is really important that this is kept secure, so that people cannot pass themselves off as you.

phishing

This is an illegal attempt by someone to try to get you to give them details of your account. Whilst it's more usual for this to be a problem with sites from Banks, and other sites with a financial interest, it is happening with social networks too.

pop-up menu

A new menu that appears when you hover over some part of the screen and that offers you new and context relevant options.

post

Posting to the site is the act of adding a single entry of information to a social networking site.

privacy settings

These are the settings that control who will be able to see the information about you, and what you are doing on the social network.

	Everyone	Friends of friends	Friends only	Other
My status, photos, and posts	•			
Bio and favorite quotations	•			
Family and relationships				•
Photos and videos I'm tagged in		•		
Religious and political views			•	

profile

Information about you that others read to help them understand what you are about as they communicate.

pull-down menu (see drop-down menu)

radio button

A button you press to show you agree with something. It's used where you can only choose one option – if one button is pressed, the others cannot be.

retweet

Twitter calls it retweeting, when you take a message that someone has sent to Twitter and you find it interesting so you send it on to your own network.

spam

Junk email or other unasked for information that gets sent to your email.

status update

Social networking sites are concerned with getting you to come back over and over again. Your status is supposed to let people know how you are right now, so should be updated frequently!

Anne Sparrowhawk I'm exploring Hootsuite at the moment which allows you to send messages to your different social networks from a single interface.

2 days ago · Like · Comment · See all activity · Post an update

tag

A tag goes onto a photograph, giving the name of the person in the photo. The person who took the photo and has ownership of the image can tag the name, but the person in the photo can usually remove that tag if they want to.

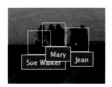

textbox

A space on the screen where you can enter information. Some can be very small, but others allow for much more extensive writing. Usually, when you have finished writing, you have to submit it for publication on screen.

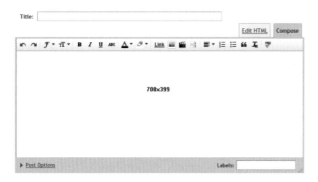

thread

A series of messages that have been discussing the same topic. As you add a message, it is added to the thread, usually at the top of the list. Sometimes it's provided as a summary at the end of the month.

Most active threads

These are the discussion threads that have had the most activity.

Programme for January concert

Dear All, the programme for our January concert (and proposed run Zanzibar Boat-Song 4. After the Fire 5. *(11 replies)*

Repertoire ideas for Summer 2011

Dear All, I'm planning a nice sunny Mediterranean repertoire for nex

A show of hands please?

Dear All, who would be interested in a participating in a small, info

Rehearsals and AGM

Dear Moonies I hope the following will make it easier for people to

thumbnail

A thumbnail is a small version of a bigger picture. It makes it easier to scan through images, and it saves you from taking a long time to download a picture you eventually realize you don't actually want.

IMG_0543   IMG_0544

IMG_0547   IMG_0548

tick box or check box

Unlike a radio button, when you are offered tick boxes, you can usually choose a number of them.

tweet

A message created on the Twitter site is called a tweet. It must be no more than 140 characters in total.

URL (see web address)

username

Most sites ask you to create a username for yourself – it does not always have to be your real name, but it's the name that you will be known by on that service.

wall

This is the term Facebook gives to your home page – the page where your information and posts appear.

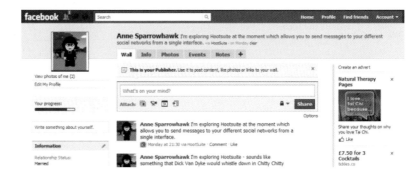

web address

The address friends who are not in the social network can be given to see your outputs.

widget

A widget is a game or piece of computer program that you can choose to add to a web page you are creating, perhaps to create a particular visual effect.

Index

M

N

O

P

R

Y